L'Atalante

2nd Edition

Marina Warner

palgrave

A BFI book published by Palgrave

For Laura and Brian with love

This edition published in 2015 by
PALGRAVE

on behalf of the

BRITISH FILM INSTITUTE
21 Stephen Street, London W1T 1LN
www.bfi.org.uk

There's more to discover about film and television through the BFI. Our world-renowned archive, cinemas, festivals, films, publications and learning resources are here to inspire you.

PALGRAVE in the UK is an imprint of Macmillan Publishers Limited, registered in England, company number 785998, of 4 Crinan Street, London N1 9XW. Palgrave Macmillan in the US is a division of St Martin's Press LLC, 175 Fifth Avenue, New York, NY 10010. Palgrave is a global imprint of the above companies and is represented throughout the world. Palgrave® and Macmillan® are registered trademarks in the United States, the United Kingdom, Europe and other countries.

Front cover design: Richey Beckett
Series text design: ketchup/SE14
Images from *L'Atalante* (Jean Vigo, 1
(Jean Vigo, 1930), Jean Vigo, Boris K

Set by couch
Printed in China

This book is printed on paper suita
forest sources. Logging, pulping an
environmental regulations of the c

British Library Cataloguing-in-Publi
A catalogue record for this book is
A catalog record for this book is av

ISBN 978–1–84457–888–7

Jean Vigo at work on *L'Atalante*, with Dita Parlo in the role of Juliette

BFI Film Classics

The BFI Film Classics is a series of books that introduces, interprets and celebrates landmarks of world cinema. Each volume offers an argument for the film's 'classic' status, together with discussion of its production and reception history, its place within a genre or national cinema, an account of its technical and aesthetic importance, and in many cases, the author's personal response to the film.

For a full list of titles available in the series, please visit our website: www.palgrave.com/bfi

'Magnificently concentrated examples of flowing freeform critical poetry.'
Uncut

'A formidable body of work collectively generating some fascinating insights into the evolution of cinema.'
Times Higher Education Supplement

'The series is a landmark in film criticism.'
Quarterly Review of Film and Video

'Possibly the most bountiful book series in the history of film criticism.'
Jonathan Rosenbaum, *Film Comment*

70001667111 6

Contents

Clos ton oeil physique afin de voir d'abord ton tableau
avec l'oeil de l'esprit.
Ensuite fais monter au jour ce que tu as vu dans la nuit.

Caspar David Friedrich, as quoted by André Breton.[1]

Foreword

It is over twenty years since I wrote this BFI Film Classic and the extraordinary quality of *L'Atalante* has not dimmed at all, eighty years since it was made; rather the opposite. The film remains a ciné-poem of luminous strangeness and poignant tenderness, constantly surprising as it moves fluidly between humour and bleakness, uncouthness and grace. Jean Vigo was able to inspire every one of the cast to give an unforgettable performance – Michel Simon as an Old Man of the Sea, Gilles Margaritis as the caddish and irresistible pedlar, Louis Lefebvre as the cabin boy, awkward in his limbs yet old beyond his years, and of course the lovers, whose shifting emotions Vigo captures with such sensitivity. Dita Parlo glows with gentle, mischievous eroticism, emitting radiance as if she were a light source in herself; Jean Dasté changes from joy to despair, as he conveys the urgency of his passion and the catatonic intensity of his loss. Vigo bound these brilliant tours de force into a compelling drama that has not lost its fascination; if anything it has gained in power for me because so few films made in recent decades have come close to its combination of delicacy and strength. It was still among the top fifty films in the 2012 *Sight & Sound* poll, in spite of the competition growing so much more numerous, and its influence persists: for example, the Pepper's Ghost apparition of Kate Moss at the end of Alexander McQueen's runway show which stunned the audience is a straight steal from – a direct tribute to – Jean's meltingly ecstatic vision of Juliette in the water.

A documentary about Vigo, made by Jacques Rozier in 1964, wasn't available to me when I wrote the essay; it's included with the most recent restoration of the film (2001), and provides a wonderfully lively and rich account of Vigo as a friend and as an artist; the interviewees were all part of 'la bande à Vigo', the

exceptionally tight-knit team who worked with him throughout his
short life, from his loyal producer Jacques Nounez, to Charles
Goldblatt, the writer of the sparkling patter song with which the
roguish pedlar enthrals Juliette. As Vigo's friends reminisce, their
affection and admiration for him beams out from the screen; words
like 'tender', 'cruel', 'madcap', 'rebellious' and 'tough' keep
recurring. Vigo was 'très rieur' – always laughing – and a 'grand
farceur' – a big prankster; his taste tended to the 'saugrenu' –
variously translated as zany, or grotesque. He always asked a great
deal of his team, and everyone gave it unconditionally: for example,
the canal was frozen when Dasté dives into it to find Juliette in the
water. But Vigo also knew how to let people be: Michel Simon
declares vehemently how he hates doing a scene twice, as the
'second time is a lie'. He remembers how Vigo understood that
and did not press him.

Their tributes reveal how Vigo loved to unleash his performers
into unscripted and playful invention, no matter how wild: the

On location in the village for the opening wedding sequence: Jean Vigo (far right)
striding next to Boris Kaufman

climactic pillow fight of *Zéro de conduite* and much of the dialogue of *L'Atalante*, especially in the scenes with le père Jules, were improvised. The result is a freshness, a sense of unforced sincerity in his films, as Vigo fuses the techniques of *vérité* documentary, which he had brought to his short films (*À propos de Nice* and *Taris: roi de l'eau*) with an auteur cinema of personal, lyric poetry and drama.

A crucial part of Vigo's brilliance lay in his gift for surrounding himself with talent, and the cinematographer Boris Kaufman is key to the unity of vision in *L'Atalante*. The restoration of 2001 brings out aspects that had faded from the version on videotape which I was working with in the l990s, and my essay doesn't give the cinematography its due. Vigo and Kaufman's camera is everywhere; it's an omniscient and ubiquitous witness, finding unexpected apertures to move through, pulling focus right into a dissolve into the back of the characters' heads, lying under Jean as he crawls towards Juliette like a cat, watching over the couple's bunk and, in one of the most yearning sequences, hanging above the young lovers and intercutting between them as they lie in different beds, dreaming of each other and spangled with the same pattern of light and shade from the glass pane in the door. The camera doesn't inhabit any of the characters' sightlines or inner processes, but roves with a mind of its own, possessed of something close to Vigo's anarchic spirit of rebellion, and accompanied by Maurice Jaubert's score, its effervescent partner in the technical dance of sound and image. Unimpeded by the constraints of the tight location, the camera travels through the interiors of the barge with extraordinary agility, up and down the companionways, into the galley and the cabins at such close quarters that we, the viewers, are caught up in the story's intimacies: we can smell the dirty laundry, the warm clean towel, le père Jules's cabin stuffed with bric-a-brac and crawling with cats and their kittens. The movements of the camera also respond to the travelling of the barge to produce one marvellously fluid sequence after another: for example, the lyrical shot of Juliette in her wedding dress walking up the barge against its direction of travel, or chronicling people high on the banks as *L'Atalante* passes by. The angles, often from above or from below, add greatly to the physicality of the vessel in which the drama is taking place: it is sometimes an ominous hulk looming above the camera, at other times, skulking low beneath the quayside, dwarfed against the stark industrial edgelands stretching to the horizon. The images give the barge an independent dramatic personality, ranging from cosiness to menace.

L'Atalante begins when a young girl leaves farmland for life on a canal barge: a transition from pastoral to urban, captured unforgettably in the abstract shapes of the conical hayricks behind the couple as they leave her village, and the vision of the cabin boy wreathed in old man's beard. Behind and beneath the love story, the film unfolds a near-documentary chronicle about labourers and industry on the waterways of northern France in the Depression: on land, a world of work – and worklessness – is made visible in magnificently framed and composed sequences. The most recent, restored print brings out the sumptuous gradations of black and silver, greys and whites of Kaufman's consummate lighting. Under Vigo's direction, Kaufman used every difficulty of circumstance – fog, steam, rain, snow, night and day, gas lamps and sunshine – to add to the poetic and emotional texture. The shoot was relentless, everyone reports, and Kaufman was always falling asleep from sheer exhaustion. But the whole crew was 'intoxicated by the scenery of the canals', remarks one witness in another documentary, *Les Voyages de L'Atalante*, made in 2001 by Eisenschitz, who gives an absorbing history of the long and troubled afterlife of *L'Atalante* from the first mangling it received in 1934 until 1990 when the BFI restored it; Eisenschitz himself worked on the 2000 version, introducing some differences in the editing. I am not expert enough to comment on the variants and decisions made by editors over the decades, and here and there – the shot of Jean licking a block of ice on the quayside – the editing still does not seem entirely sure.

Not long before Kaufman and Vigo worked together on

À propos de Nice (l930), Kaufman had made *Les Halles centrale* (1927), about the historic central market of Paris, celebrated for its porters and traders. The visual language of *L'Atalante* is also shaped by Russian revolutionary aesthetics about modernity, cities and working men and women. It conveys their relations to their surroundings in formal constructivist compositions: derricks, chimneys, cranes, gantries and pylons, silhouetted, sombrely lit or drifting with mist, tower over men and women, who are often crushed in scale by contrast. At the start, Juliette finds life on the barge involves a daily grind and no fun, but as the film develops, the vessel gradually becomes a sanctuary and a promise of escape, as the last, aerial shot of a vast empty tract of water into which it is ascending communicates so eloquently.

This socialist political consciousness, pulsing underneath the sensitive romance of the film, was shared by everyone in Vigo's band of friends working with him on the film. When I wrote the essay all those years ago, I deliberately kept back, until the very end, the devastating story of his childhood, of his parents' anarchist activities, their pacifism, and his father's repeated jail sentences, and his death in prison, probably murdered. I did not want the tragedy of Vigo's life to provide the dominant lens through which we saw the film. There is a famous moment in John Berger's *Ways of Seeing* when he presents a painting by Van Gogh of a cornfield, and then reveals that it is the last work of the painter before he killed himself. Berger is interested in conveying how this information changes the whole effect and meaning of Van Gogh's picture: the field with birds fluttering down becomes charged with foreboding and tragedy. When you learn that Jean Vigo was twenty-nine when he was making *L'Atalante* and had been suffering from TB since he was a boy, and that he died of complications of his illness (rheumatic septicaemia) before he saw the final cut of his masterpiece, the knowledge of this tragic history overshadows the entire film, turning it into a swansong, its maker into the Rimbaud of cinema, his oeuvre a poignant elegy for what might have been.

I am still generally opposed to reading a novel or viewing a film through the biography of the writer, director or stars, but I admit that it's often impossible now to keep them separate: Marilyn Monroe's tragic end adds powerfully twisted feelings – irony, regret, compassion, curiosity – to her entrancing presence on screen, especially in her bubbly comic roles. Looking at *L'Atalante* in the light of what we know about Jean Vigo's short life does deepen the power of the film's testimony to love, to the depths of joy and pain that it brings. Vigo knew he had little to no time left when he was making it, and he wanted to say something important about the ordinary things that matter. It presents us with his belief in intimacy and friendship, spontaneity and delight, hope and love. That he succeeded so magnificently was the consequence of his unique and marvellous gifts, and we continue to be inestimably enriched.

It was the troubadours from Provence who first evoked the ideal of le gai saber – the phrase which was taken up by Nietzsche in the title of his book *The Gay Science*. It has since acquired a different patina, but the evolution of gay rights also keeps in mind the earlier meaning: *joie de vivre* as well as intense pleasure in curiosity and discovery – in knowledge. Vigo's oeuvre is filled with that irrepressible gaiety, that energy of appetite for life and experience that can transform the humdrum into the transcendent. He has influenced some of the greatest film-makers – Truffaut, Fellini. May his spirit live on, may he continue to inspire poets, dreamers, makers of cinema!

Marina Warner
Princeton Institute for Advanced Study
Easter 2015

Acknowledgments

The author wishes to thank Sally Potter, who generously shared her original insights into Vigo's work. Much thanks, too, to the British Film Institute and its staff, especially in the Library and the projection rooms. Colin MacCabe, Duncan Petrie, John Gillett and Esther Johnson helped make the post of Visiting Fellow in 1992 highly enjoyable as well as inspiring and productive; without David Meeker's help, nobody could venture to write about *L'Atalante*. She is very grateful to them all for help and advice. The credits were checked by Markku Salmi.

Prologue

The erotic spectacle has become commonplace; a graphic language of rapture – naked bodies, deep kissing and (the new figleaf shot) rumpy-pumpy – has been naturalised over the last twenty years to represent love-making on the screen. Though such pictures of sex stimulate feelings – envy as well as lust – in me, the sight of a couple doing it somehow doesn't add up to an erotic experience of the same degree as the film *Lucia* (1968) gave me, or *Rashomon* (1950). Or *L'Atalante*. I'm not declaring myself against nudity in the movies. But I am proposing that the visual record of couplings has its affective limits, and that film, like music, and, even more particularly, like jazz, can sometimes express longing, desire, promise, fear of loss and all the other components of erotic love in images that reach out to symbolise the act, rather than to render it in forthright pictures. The problem is: to develop such metaphors requires the kind of imaginative and expressive energy few people have; anyone (almost) can sing 'Lover Come Back to Me'. But Billie Holiday sings it with a difference.

Although by no means all the lyrics someone like Billie Holiday sang were banal, her capacity to voice passion wasn't damaged when they were. Sounds and movements in-between words, in-between syllables express the emotion and convey sincerity and force – not what the mother of the child killed in a civil war is saying, even through an interpreter, but how she draws in her breath and screws up her eyes. And in the language of cinema, sounds in-between play a crucial part too, of course, as they combine with the passage of images telling the story. But again, the emotional atmosphere of a film doesn't rise fully from the tagged moments of narrative development, the numbered scenes on the shooting script, but from the moments in-between, sometimes visible images, but not always. A juxtaposition in a montage can yield a meaning that does not have to be represented or take apprehensible form to make itself present: the invisible, implied picture.

L'Atalante is a romance. When Jean Vigo was first given the script by Jean Guinée (the pseudonym of Roger de Guichen), he protested. 'Mais qu'est-ce que tu veux que je foute avec ça, c'est un scénario pour patronage?' ('What the fuck do you want me to do with this – it's Sunday school stuff').[2] It is indeed a banal story – in content nothing special, in structure predictable; even the characters' names seem the first to hand, so casual that they fail to register even as emblematic: Jean for the bargee, Juliette for the bride he brings on board, le père Jules for his henchman; the third member of the crew remains anonymous, 'le gosse' (the boy). The story has little to it. After a while, Juliette becomes dissatisfied with life on the barge and plays truant in Paris; Jean, in a huff, sails off without waiting for her to return, and falls into distraction and despair; at last, le père Jules sets out to bring her back and does so. But some things happen which undo the banality – and the thinness – of this story, and their very realisation reveals the fundamental error of confusing the ordinary with the unremarkable, entertainment with eventfulness. For it is often poverty of imagination that spins a great foam of dramatic incident in which to hide; richness that allows the banal its beauty.

René Clair remarks in his reminiscences that to him cinema was a medium of dreaming.[3] Words did not matter, only pictures, and the spectator became a dreamer, carried along on the images' suggestiveness. Vigo was an admirer of René Clair, and when his friend and co-writer Albert Riéra, on behalf of the producer Jacques-Louis Nounez, pointed out to him he could make something of *L'Atalante*, he may have agreed for this reason. With Riéra, he began to work on a revision of Guinée's maudlin original.

L'Atalante tells one of the most tender and convincing love stories on film; John Grierson, among the rare critics to appreciate it from the beginning, perceptively wrote at the time:

He [Vigo] tells it in a style peculiar to himself. It is an exciting style. At the base of it is a sense of documentary realism which makes the barge a real barge. ... But on top of the realism is a crazy Vigo world of symbols and magic. ... The Mate, too, more monstrously, represents romance. It is a novel and fascinating way of story-telling, and Vigo is clearly one of the most imaginative young directors in Europe.[4]

Romance, in its earliest surviving form, was called 'erotika pathemata' by the Greeks – tales of erotic suffering. After initial bliss and consummation, the lovers passed through a period of trials; temptations, as well as ordeals, tested their love, until at last they were reunited and their love was free to begin as the story came to its traditional happy ending. The story of Cupid and Psyche (Love and the Soul) emerged as the template of the genre in the Renaissance, though it is embedded in the metaphysical, seriocomic Latin novel *The Golden Ass* by Apuleius, who was writing in the second century AD.[5]

Nothing could be more commonplace than a romance; nothing could be more resistant, it would appear at a first glance, to deep examination or lasting statement, to magical transformation. Banality and sentiment, entrenched reactionariness in class and sexual politics and queasy wishfulness clog the genre in most of its contemporary manifestations, from deodorant and perfume ads to bodice-ripper yarns. Yet *L'Atalante* is a traditional romance. It follows a journey of the heart for both protagonists, itself replicated in the slow travelling of the barge down the canal between Le Havre and Corbeil, south of Paris, and back to Le Havre, via the metropolitan docks at La Villette. Five times Jean loses Juliette, at first in his mind, later in reality – her gentleness is tested by his roughness, his tenderness bruised by her volatility, and both learn the depths of their need and their passion for each other; she is open to temptations, he is impatient; she desires the world beyond the barge, he has closed it off. Though this tale of erotic suffering unfolds without loss of intensity, its poignancy pulses through a coat of many colours, made of humour, dreams, fantasy, street acts, songs, mischievous wit, surprise and improvisation. Like the genre of Greek and medieval romance, the film refuses to segregate serious and comic matters, high style and low, the physical and the metaphysical, the apparent and the inward. This refusal nevertheless finds expression through the realist vision of the moving camera, in a flow of unselfconscious, unaffected, fluent images of the manifest world, in the interior, domestic details of work and the unadorned scenery of industrial labour.

Truffaut commented that it was one of those films 'qui sent les pieds' ('whose feet smell').[6] This proved an unfamiliar aesthetic experience, hence unpopular when L'Atalante was first screened: the old anarchist and writer Georges de La Fouchardière, a friend of Vigo's father, was heard to go out muttering, 'lavatory flushings'. But this lack of squeamishness translates into stylistic energy of a quality that has not dated, when other, more evasive image-making looks stilted (for instance, Vigo's contemporary, the writer-cinéaste Marcel Pagnol, with his studies of Marseilles working people in César [1936]). Vigo's combination of fantasy and naturalness has kept L'Atalante from becoming a mere locus of trite, nostalgic gallicisms about 'l'amour' and 'le bon coeur des gens'.

How does L'Atalante avoid the sentimentality that dogs romance? It does so at various levels: through effervescent invention, a wayward storyline, the ironical counterpoint of giddy music and painful experience, and a quality of sincere innocence which the principals succeed in portraying. But there is also a formal explanation, which relates to the narrative techniques of the tale in literature as well. Vigo does not use the camera in lieu of a person. He does not tend to align the viewpoint with the sightlines of his characters; seldom do we see what Jean or Juliette is seeing. There are certain occasions – when Jean and Juliette first arrive at the dance hall, we see the entrance from their joint angle. Later, we window-gaze with Juliette in Paris. But generally the camera observes from its own position, which has been chosen to create an image, not to enter the subjectivity of a character; the image then carries the mood, the meaning, the impact of the scene, not the imputed feelings of one of the participants. Even in the film's climactic vision, when Juliette appears in the water, the next shot does not show Jean reciprocating this miracle with an answering smile, but rather shows him still as it were blinded underwater, and we, in the audience, who have seen Juliette, cannot be sure if he has also seen her. The camera is not in his head or seeing with his eyes.

In its independence, the camera approximates to the conventional unattached voice of the storyteller of folklore, who does not use the first person, or bear witness through a third-person voice with whom she or he identifies, but maintains a formal difference, which reduces affect. In the act of restraining sympathy and displays of emotional sympathy, this cool kind of narrator who unfolds the story without declaring partisanship manages to pull at the audience's feelings more powerfully. *L'Atalante*'s camera does not need to stick with Jean, or Juliette or le père Jules's ways of telling the story. This freedom allows Vigo many registers of feeling – he can vary the mood independently of the characters' involvement, he can observe Jean's despair, Juliette's curiosity, with a kind of precision that isn't fogged by sentiments of disapproval or loyalty. The camera's autonomy creates a stylistic richness, aesthetically and emotionally, which many of today's films fail to achieve as their directors desperately strive for narrative logic by keeping the camera in line with a character's point of view in plodding shots one way, followed by a reverse-angle shot the other. *L'Atalante* contains many mysterious images, non-sequiturs and peculiar moments. I wouldn't go so far as the critic Terrence Rafferty, who pointed out,

The best thing about this new version is that, for all the restorer's diligence, the film is still messy, imperfect, defiantly incomplete: it's a collection of inspired fragments, the sketchbook of an artist whose imagination was, and will forever remain, gloriously immature.[7]

I read Vigo's imprint more definitely on the material. He was inventing his cinema aesthetic as he went along, and it is a great shame that in spite of his fame he has not had a huge influence. Like Matisse, he's an artist who inspires everyone who has looked at him, but has no obvious successful emulators.

Vigo also avoids mawkishness by rebuffing morality. The film isn't a goody-goody film even though it is about love, marriage and reconciliation. Vigo made fundamental changes in this respect. Guinée had ended the original synopsis with the ominous words: 'Mais le Bonheur a fui le bord' ('But Happiness had left the ship') – the marriage will never be the same after Juliette's truancy.[8] Vigo's film of course contradicts this spirit of doom, and his happy ending resoundingly defies despair. Guinée could have been influenced by a nineteenth-century Grand Guignol play called *La Houppelande* (*The Cape*), which dramatised a love triangle on a barge and ended in the murder of the lover by the husband. Puccini had been inspired by it to compose his short opera *Il tabarro*, which was first performed in New York in 1918, and it's not impossible that Jean Guinée had heard it. The canal setting – in northern France – and the agony of the husband that he is going to lose his wife strike very similar notes; the gloomy moralising of his original script also shares something in common with Puccini, even though it does not end in the melodrama of *crime passionnel*.[9] Vigo's complete transformation of pessimism into hope fulfils the conditions of classical romance, of course, but it also proposes a modern strategy to the dilemmas of life and love, as opposed to morbidity and misogyny.

Paradoxically, his romance represents a turning away from romanticism.

L'Atalante: the first three shots

'L'Atalante'

The wedding

The first shot shows the stern of the barge and 'L'Atalante', her name, painted on the hull. The barge is the film and they share a woman's name. With spare economy this opening image sets the scene of struggle, about love and the place of women: where they choose to be, where they are contained. The viewer's eye is then concentrated on a smaller point of visual interest: the reflection of water, winking on the rim. A precise eye for graphic beauty landed on that bead of dancing light – and it foreshadows *L'Atalante*'s imagery throughout. Boris Kaufman was Vigo's lighting cameraman on all his films – he shared director's credit for *À propos de Nice* – and his handling of shape through light and shadow clearly contributed in a major way to *L'Atalante*'s wonderful lucidity of image.

The film never sentimentalises the working life of the bargees, but it presents their surroundings with unfailing respect, creating, out of the smoky, damp winter of the canals, a subtle geometry and a moody, austere aesthetic. The first shot also anticipates one of Vigo's most characteristic artistic resources: the light bounces off the water, which itself doesn't command the viewer's attention, as it is eclipsed by the greater value of the hull and the name inscribed on it. Throughout the film, the four edges of the frame are always dissolved to suggest what is visible beyond them, to stimulate the viewer's own powers of visualisation and bring into play the world the camera's rectangular sights cannot encompass – here, the rest of the barge, the banks and the flow of the canal, where a boat glides by in the background. Because this style of framing implies the world beyond its borders, Vigo can approach his subjects obliquely, swiftly, suggestively, with pans passing the backs of heads, the set of a pair of shoulders, the motion of passing feet, a shadow in a corner.

The first shot of the film is held, unusually for Vigo, before it cuts to a view of the canal and the barge lying in it, but the screen soon fills up with a head of steam – exhaled from an undisclosed source lying beneath the whole baseline of the image. Only much later, and fleetingly in the background, do we see the sort of passing freight train which might have breathed out this great cloud. Significantly, *Zéro de conduite* (1933) opens with a cloud of steam rising behind the carriage window in the railway compartment. It's a signal of departure, like the first letting out of pent-up excitement before entering the stage. The rising steam of *L'Atalante*'s second shot also indicates beginnings under pressure, and even hints at the release of passionate feelings. It is one of those images in-between, the marrow of montage, where the symbolic and the real coexist as enigma. It doesn't linger, either, for Vigo's way of telling makes quick, light footfalls – he isn't a stickler for causal linkage.

A steeply raked view of a church next appears, to the continued dud tolling of a bell; the skew-whiff angle and the image's still, impersonal vacancy introduce the first note of oddness, and this will gradually gather force as the first scene develops, showing the wedding procession making its way from the church to the barge. Le père Jules, the ship's mate (Michel Simon), appears, scurrying through the church door; he's holding the boy (Louis Lefebvre, from *Zéro de conduite*) by the hand, yanking him along. They're dressed identically, with black bow ties and caps; the formal attire looks ill-fitting, unaccustomed. Suddenly, le père Jules lollops back to the church to cross himself with holy water. His simian gait matches his prognathous jaw, while a double shadow against the wall casts an uneasy question over his brutish behaviour. The married couple, Jean and Juliette, come out of church and turn in the direction the ship's mate has taken. A crocodile of guests forms behind them, but not tidily enough for one of the men present, who later bosses them into regular pairs. Juliette's mother, in front, is crying over her daughter's departure with an outsider. 'And to think she's never left the village before,' she whimpers. Someone complains there's to be no wedding banquet; but another explains that the bridegroom is in a hurry to catch up on his delivery job for the canal freight company; another mentions that he's a stranger and that Juliette didn't consider a local man was good enough. The procession's absurdity stirs echoes of social satire – the bowler hat, which the male guests are all wearing, was a favourite Surrealist symbol of stuffiness, of course, targeted not only in the art of Max Ernst and Magritte, but also in burlesque movies like Hans Richter's *Ghosts Before Breakfast* (1928) where hats waft about in a solemn procession on their own. Though in *L'Atalante* the dialogue is barely audible, it helps set up an important theme: Juliette is leaving the familiar for the unfamiliar, her *Heimat*, as it were, for the unknown.

Human contact is peremptory, chilly; the mood perplexingly sombre for a wedding. Doubts about Jean are seeded in the viewer's mind, anxiety about Juliette. The bridal pair move fast, arm in arm, mechanically advancing, looking straight ahead, stiff and unsmiling;

The married couple

they begin to gain ground over the wedding party, who seem almost to be shuffling along reluctantly, behind the newly-weds, in widow's weeds and mourners' headgear. The bell does not peal, but tolls arhythmically, as if the wind were taking it, under the squeezebox jollity of two guests, and later, on the soundtrack, a haunting, reedy tune, as Jean and Juliette, still like wind-up toys, walk briskly across a field; they're seen alone, small, against hayricks, then again, closer, in tall weeds; then again, abruptly, against the furrows; still they make no eye or speech contact, and the only light glows from her satin wedding dress. Sally Potter, the director, chose *L'Atalante* as one of her top ten films in 1992, and she observes that Vigo creates 'a metaphysical dimension' by handling the depth of field in a manner he learned from Eisenstein. Figures move far and near through space in the film in an expressive way, in which their relation to the space itself becomes queered.[10]

The oddness of the opening also springs from another factor that lies beyond the control of Vigo and his collaborators in 1934. The shot of the wedding pair in the distance against three conical haystacks possesses that clarity of formal arrangement associated with still photographers of the first part of the century of whom both Vigo and Kaufman were fully acquainted. It is one of the shots that was reintroduced into *L'Atalante* when the film was restored, in 1990, by Gaumont. It is, needless to say, a beautiful – and characteristic – shot which works for the scene's meaning. The haystacks are pillowy, their sculpted contours sensuously textured, and the wedding pair look small and vulnerable against their strength and composure. The image of Jean and Juliette in tall grass which follows immediately is also one of the restored shots – kept 'for the beauty of the images', the Gaumont press brochure declares.[11] Independently beautiful, sequentially jangling, the shots disrupt the narrative logic, implausibly prolonging the walk from the village to the barge over untrodden terrain. The effect is powerful, but it isn't certain that in the original 1934 cut the sequence would have been so unsettling.

The wedding procession then cuts to the ship's mate, who's rehearsing the boy's lines to welcome the bride. The boy's nasal singsong, 'Heureuse vie à bord de l'Atalante', promises badly; he seems half-witted, pitching his performance nearer pathos than comedy. The peculiar, lugubrious sense of menace increases.

On the barge, the old man, a kitten riding clutched on his shoulders, botches his plan to present a bouquet when the boy kicks it overboard in the middle of a brief hornpipe – this first, small sign of joy ends in curses from the old salt Jules, and an ominous mutter that God isn't on their side. The raw dialogue, filled with repetitions, and deliberately coarse in accent and phrasing (Michel Simon's Vaudois brogue helps), strikes the ear as utterly different from any other film of the 1930s in its unrehearsed naturalism. When the boy runs off to pick some wild flowers instead, he returns, in a low-angle shot with delicately luminous lighting, haloed in a great mass of traveller's joy against the banked clouds. He gives the bride, his new *patronne*, the scrawny, limp bouquet retrieved from

'Haloed in a great mass of traveller's joy'

the water, and Jean and Juliette smile – at him, but not at each other. Jean immediately leaves Juliette on her own as he leaps into action on the barge. Juliette stands alone, on land, below him, her lids heavy, her brow furrowed, to all appearances utterly forlorn.

Le père Jules swings Juliette over the gap between the bank and the barge on the boom; her mother runs down the bank after her, but it is too late – she's crossed over without a proper goodbye, and her mother finds herself in the arms of the old man instead, who thrusts the bunch of flowers at her. It could be a funny moment, but remains funny-peculiar, too. At the levers of the engine, Jean throws his cap in the air and shouts goodbye, leaping up and down. His gesture, given the overall feeling of foreboding, seems inappropriate, entirely insensitive to the mood of the gathering. On the shore, the mother stands apart in front of the crowd. Nobody on the bank responds; massed together, seen from the point of view of the barge from above, they observe Juliette's departure without a smile or a cheer. At the bows, she stands alone –

Juliette: 'shot of premonitory eeriness'

a shot of premonitory eeriness, as the sound of the engine gathers speed on the soundtrack.

The entire atmosphere evokes a funeral, not a wedding – the shadowy lighting, the coffin-like box of the barge, the expressionless guests and the drowned bouquet. The inconsequent jumps from village to field to meadow give the wedding march a spooky, jumbled feel, and when the boy looms, wreathed in trailing wild flowers, the film touches not only on fairy tales in which the young bride is given to a dark and disturbing stranger, as in 'Bluebeard' or 'Beauty and the Beast', but on myths about spring brides and lords of the underworld. It's overdetermining the imagery to interpret Juliette as Persephone and Jean as Pluto who carries her off – it's tantamount to hauling Vigo on to Cocteau territory, where the symbols announce themselves by name and a heightened, learned aesthetic serves the mythic message. In *L'Atalante*, the mythic resonances sound much farther away: the material texture of ordinary contemporary existence occupies the foreground. Nevertheless, they do sound.

These illogical leaps in *L'Atalante*'s opening montage carry the audience out of rural Normandy into unpredictable territory, a closed kingdom where her companions will be this grim crew of joyless husband, ruffianly hand, and loutish boy. There's also something sacrificial about Juliette as she stands, faltering, at the prow; she stirs memories of maidens offered up to the sea to appease monsters, of effigies fixed to bowsprits to protect the ship.

The title of the film comes from the original script. Atalanta was an Amazonian heroine who challenged her suitors to a footrace; unless they could outstrip her, she refused them (in some versions, she killed them) – until a certain Melanion trapped her by throwing down golden apples before her as she ran. Curiosity – so often the principle of fate in myths about women – was her undoing as she stopped to investigate them, and Melanion was able to pass her and win the race. In some tellings, he had already caught her fancy, so when she slowed to pick up the balls she only did so because she had relented from her celibacy and wanted him to win.

(*next page*) The skies are louring and Juliette fearful as she embarks on her new life with Jean on board 'L'Atalante'

Jean Guinée had been inspired to write the script by the sight one day of a woman at the helm of a barge on the Seine – a kind of modern-day Amazon of sorts, perhaps. However, he had chosen to give the boat – and the film – this particular name because an ancestor in his family, the admiral de Guichen, had sailed in a frigate called 'L'Atalante' in the American War of Independence. It's a grand pedigree for a freight barge, but it carries, interestingly, connotations that do linger on even in Vigo's thorough recasting of Guinée's script: themes of struggle, of courage and of female conflicts about dependence in love remain in the film. Guinée's script actually makes the suggestion that when Juliette comes aboard and takes up her position at the bow, she should look like a traditional figurehead. He intended an overlap between the heroine of the Greek myth and the new wife of the bargee, and Vigo kept it.

The objection might be made that Vigo or his co-adaptor Albert Riéra are unlikely to have known Guinée's private reasons for calling the script *L'Atalante*, and that the robust freshness of Vigo's film-making arises from his complete disregard for such schoolroom style of thinking. But echoes that are not consciously intended and consequently are not controlled by the author are struck by works in all media in unison with the image store of its receivers. *L'Atalante* would be a different film under a different name – if it were called, for instance, 'La Louis XVI', which was the actual name of the barge hired for the filming. Apart from having a supple, graceful shape, the word 'L'Atalante' is feminine in gender, which helps define the dominant place of struggle in the film. Jean suffers, of course, but the story is above all the struggle in Juliette, over giving herself totally to love-in-marriage.

At close quarters

The knell from the church has stopped, and a Maurice Jaubert tune, dominated by the melancholy, velvet playing of a saxophone, takes over on the soundtrack to accompany images of Jean and Juliette's first moments of intimacy. The rather dry, staccato motions of the wedding sequence now begin to give way to a liquid, gliding movement, as the camera scans the bank or passes over the barge and follows the movements of the protagonists, often in contraflow to the direction of the boat itself. Underscoring the fateful mood, two shots of the land Juliette has left are interwoven with her arrival on board: a single house looms on the quay, as if seen from the point of view of the low-lying barge. The lights come on in two windows: night apparently has already fallen. When Juliette stands at the prow, we see Jean come up and put his arms around her from behind. Instantly, she falls back inertly into his arms; he lays her down on the deck. A cat suddenly jumps onto them as he's kissing her neck, and she springs abruptly to life, and struggles away from him. Her wreath falls off, but she returns for it to fasten her bridal veil back in place. The retrieval implies her inability to accept that she must relinquish her bridal costume, itself a crystallisation of the unblemished world of girlhood. Indeed, when Jean lowers her on to the deck, the viewer feels a sympathetic fear of being dirtied – the soft white satin she's wearing has been glowing in the dark, after all.

Her garland back in place, Juliette begins to walk against the direction of the barge's motion, away from Jean in the prow towards the stern – a spectral figure alone on the grey-black fuselage of the boat against the dark pooling water of the canal. It is one of the most haunting images in the film. Then, much nearer, indeed far nearer than could be seen from the angle of Juliette or anyone else on board, a shrouded woman and a child glide into vision, like Breton Calvary pilgrims, ominously lit from below. The woman makes the sign of the cross – as if the barge were a passing hearse and an apotropaic gesture was needed rather than a blessing on newly-weds. The contradictory camera movements in this sequence – the woman and child glide past in reverse direction to the barge – 'undermine all sense of stability and fixedness', creating 'a hallucinatory quality'.[12]

Jean follows Juliette along the top of the barge, but whereas she had picked her way cautiously over the looped cable in the

middle, he trips over it in his eagerness. Cats – and kittens – again
spring at his face, where he has fallen, startling him and scratching
his cheek; the attack makes Juliette relent, and she kisses him, for
the first time, impetuously. He picks her up, in the traditional
posture of the bridegroom carrying his wife over the threshold; she
nestles up against his neck, kittenishly squirming and laughing, her
dress now fluttering up. The tension between them has evaporated
all of a sudden, and the first shaft of the radiance that makes itself
felt every now and then throughout the film breaks in as Jean
begins to take Juliette down into the interior of the barge. Jean, still
carrying her, walks out of shot, and the picture fades – for the first
time in the movie.

The barge

The barge will be Juliette's home, the whole of her new country as
a married woman; like Psyche in the classical romance, she cannot
leave its confines. In many traditional fairy tales of the Beauty and
the Beast type, the heroine has to adjust to her new home, the
strange place where her mysterious husband rules. In many ways,
the barge is a modern avatar of the Beast's castle.

Bargee life had fed a small stream of early French realism in the
cinema: Jean Epstein's *La Belle Nivernaise* (1923) and Jean Renoir's
La Fille de l'eau (1924) both featured life on the industrial canals of
northern France.[13] The barge, as a uniquely unified space, a modern
castle where a hero and a heroine must be tried, offered possibilities
L'Atalante seizes with unsurpassed imaginative energy. It encloses its
inhabitants in a definite way; there are few windows, the hatches
close over their heads, the view from on board, as Juliette says later,
consists only of 'les rives', the banks. In *L'Atalante*, no glimmer of
pastorale alleviates the austere landscape of warehouses, cranes,
telegraph poles – an industrial wilderness. Artificial waterways,
unnaturally straight and controlled with machinery and locks, canals
also suggest discipline and authority; their purposefulness contrasts
with a natural river's meander, their measured levels with natural

currents' flux; the barge must run straight in its groove, obediently. *L'Atalante* builds on this image in two directions: the film sketches a social realist narrative of employees and tough management in the background, and in the foreground dramatises with exceptional sensitivity how two young people manage to adapt to the regulatory condition of living together.

The compact interior of a barge forces intimacy, desired or not, and fosters the quick development of close encounters. Vigo had an exact model of the inside of the barge made in the studio, and he filmed in it, only very rarely flying a wall or removing a partition – hence the camera often hangs above the action or shoots from tight angles in the rooms, from below, or from the side, as its subjects move in and out of the frame. Contact between people on board when inside the cabins is frequent, but never casual. *L'Atalante* is a study of eros, and at certain moments a memorably

Eugène Atget, 'Un coin du quai de la Tournelle' (1911)

erotic film; not through the spectacle of touch – what a caress or a kiss looks like – so much as its continual attention to the effects of contact. The after-images left by tactile pleasure or pain – affect that takes place to the side of the action – behave like hyphens, lying in-between one act of contact and another. There is some remarkable punctuation of this kind in the narrative throughout the film, and it first occurs in the action and after-effect of the cats – of the many cats and kittens on board the barge.

The Guinée script specified a dog, the more familiar pet of barge life, but Vigo brought in many cats – the largest number in a single scene seems to be six – from a stray animals' home. His own childhood had been populated with cats, as his father was extremely fond of them. The first kitten in *L'Atalante* appears perched on the burly shoulders of le père Jules; as a pirate of the internal man-made waterways, he sports a domestic animal in lieu of a parrot. He shows himself completely oblivious to the little

The first kitten in *L'Atalante*

animal gripping onto his jacket, so oblivious that he's clearly wholly at one with it. It's his animal familiar: a tight relationship between man and nature, between creatures of different species, which the personality of the old ship's mate, brought to life in Michel Simon's performance, will develop with unforgettable vividness.

The scratching of Jean's face melts Juliette's resistance the first night on board; the next day, Jean plays a cat, crawling towards Juliette on all fours, smiling, and passes right over the camera on his way, so that we become one with Juliette, and feel with her when she first emerges from the hatch, glowing with sleepy sensuousness. The hostility and menace of their wedding day have been dissipated and gentle, playful tenderness between them takes their place, as Jean whispers in her ear and we watch her smiling at what she hears (which we cannot). Their new-found reciprocity is convincing, relaxing the earlier foreboding of the audience. This ogre may be a softie after all. But the new sunniness in the air is soon interrupted when Jean crossly calls le père Jules to see what one of his cats has done: she has littered in the couple's own double bed. This delights the mate; he coos with pleasure. But Juliette and Jean aren't forgiving: the cats' birth amounts in their eyes to an excess of animal energy, a surplus of nature – and trespass. The kittens do not rouse sentimental responses in either of the young marrieds nor prompt dreams of fertility, as might be expected. Le père Jules catches the human implications, for – in a flash of comedy – he protests that he's hardly to blame as he's not the father. Then, when he scoops up the cat and her kittens, he grumbles that Jean is so hard-hearted he'd drown his own offspring. The dialogue plays on the double meaning of *bête* (animal and stupid), and it is the old man alone who is human and clever enough to span the rift between animal nature and human – not the young lovers. Later, his deckhand, the boy, also falls with a cry of joy on the sight of the new kittens; he too has the capacity for spontaneous affection.

Dirty washing

When Truffaut wrote that *L'Atalante* was the kind of film whose
feet smell, he was picking up on certain scenes of unprecedented
frankness. Immediately after the birth of the new kittens to le père
Jules's collection, Juliette opens the cupboard in their bedroom
cabin and out falls a year's worth of dirty washing, or so she
exclaims. Without a hint of faltering, she announces she'll do the
laundry, while Jean tries to kick it back into the cupboard. The boy
is told to fetch his own, and the old man's as well.

The atmosphere of danger which gathered over Juliette's arrival as
the new wife no longer clusters around Jean; it has shifted balance, and
the ship's mate now seems to pose the greatest problem for Juliette's
happiness on board 'L'Atalante'. He opposes her offer to do his laundry
with sarcastic repetitions of her formal position, as *la patronne* (the
missus). Her presence has made him lose caste, his disgruntled
behaviour implies. He mutters sarcastically that he's there to do anything
for her, that he'll even run errands to the shops for her. During this
passage, the film veers dangerously towards becoming a dull domestic
comedy about an incoming wife's difficulties in establishing her
authority – something Guinée's script certainly had in its sights.

A scrap merchant, dubbed Raspoutine after his big black
beard, whistles from the bank – he has a record for le père Jules
(later, it turns out to be a magic gift). Jean is helping Juliette with
the laundry, and has taken his shirt off; the light plays delectably on
his bare skin and fine shoulders, and they ply the handle of the old
wringer together, singing away at the 'Chanson des mariniers', with
its merry chorus, about honest toil on board:

On n'est pas sur les penich' pour s'balader
Faut turbiner
Jamais quitter la barre
Se coucher toujours tard
Se lever toujours tôt
Prendre soin du bateau ...[14]

Soon after this merry-making at the laundry tub, one of Vigo's most poetic and inspiring innovations utterly transforms the rather humdrum material. Jean bends to rinse his face in the bucket, and Juliette suddenly pushes his head down and holds it there for a moment. Again, contact between people is brusque, turbulent, raw. But the aftermath of this turns into a vision of piercing sweet mischief, opening a new, internal dimension of dream in the realistic exterior fabric of the film so far.

Juliette demands, in mock expostulation, why Jean closed his eyes under the water, when she held his head down. She tells him that you can see the one you love if you keep your eyes open and that, as a girl, she used to play those kinds of games with her friends. That's how, when he came to her home for the first time, she had recognised him. (The English subtitles here fail to catch the colloquial pell-mell of Juliette's speech.) As in the game of cherry stones or skipping rhymes, the beloved's identity can be magically

Jean helps Juliette with the laundry

discovered under water.[15] Jean's response is unexpectedly ardent; he throws himself into the game, and when he fails in the bucket, impetuously jumps into the dinghy and thrusts his head into the opaque canal, three times shouting up at last to Juliette, who's on the deck protesting at his ardour, 'I see you, I see you!' But it seems he sees her in real life only, not in magic – and in Vigo, the eyes of imagination report the more important truth than the eyes of the body.

L'Atalante handles the moment lightly, bubbling with all Dita Parlo's effervescent sweetness in the role. Yet the exchange sketches a lover's test Jean has failed, as in a romance of chivalry; only the true lover, her game implies, will pass it. The superstition – the fancy – reverberates with many overtones of enchantment: with the legends of the grail, which can only be seen by a pure knight, and even with diviner's cups, in which the water reflects the future. But none of this becomes falsely lyrical or self-consciously poetic: it takes place against a backdrop of a large square warehouse, and the acting stays punchy and immediate throughout. Then Jean flings himself up again onto the barge where Juliette is hanging out the laundry, and she gives chase; when he catches her, they play, and back to back, arms linked, they lift each other off the deck, chuckling, a hybrid creature.

Their lovers' frolic inspires le père Jules (who has returned to the boat with an enormously elaborate wall-mounted arrangement of horseshoes) to demonstrate that you do not need to be two people to invoke fantastic couplings. Lying under the laundry line, he shows different wrestling holds; superimposed one upon the other, figures of le père Jules multiply, but when he stops, his audience has gone and he finds himself alone. 'Les cochons!' ('The pigs'), he grumbles. The coquetry over the chores leads to more tenderness – down in their cabin, Juliette promises Jean that he will see her one day underwater when he does it for real. In the 1990 documentary made to introduce the new edit of *L'Atalante*, there's a shot of Dita Parlo impulsively kissing Jean's back, but sadly it's still missing from the film, which cuts instead to her holding a shirt from the stove to her cheek and giving it to him. 'Tiens, c'est bien chaud, ça' ('Here, it's nice and warm'). Again, the informality of the speech contributes to the feeling of intimacy, that no one is there but the two of them together. He hugs her tightly and backs her into the camera.

Much of the power of these inconsequential domestic scenes of intimacy on board 'L'Atalante' on the first day of their marriage arises from qualities in Dita Parlo which will become more and more important in the course of the film. Few close-ups of her face occur at the start, but they will become more intense as the story of loss gathers strength and speed. Mood shifts take place unexplained from moment to moment. From the dissolve as Jean takes Juliette in his arms and backs her into their room and the lens, the film cuts to Juliette, alone in bed, waking to the sound of the engine grinding, the rain battering the barge; she calls Jean down, 'It's five in the morning', but he pays no attention, grimly clutching the controls in streaming sou'wester and mackintosh. This marks the beginning of her growing dissatisfaction with the constraints of barge life, and the closest close-up of her face so far fills the screen with her dejection: Dita Parlo hooded-eyed, an expression from the era of silent melodrama.

The next day she hears the radio call, 'Ici Paris', and the announcer, in a metropolitan chant, gives details of the latest fashions; Jean rebuffs her curiosity in irritation. But she's not so easily restrained. He senses danger, and that night experiences his most vivid presentiment that he might lose her. The barge is travelling through dense fog, to the stray hoots of other boats and the urgent clanging of the bell by Jean. There's a near-collision with another barge; the confusion increases the general feeling of being lost. Juliette has come up on deck, and sits huddled in the drifting mist, brooding; Jean finds their cabin empty and cries out for her. She refuses to answer. He feels his way like a sleepwalker along the boat until he finds her, seizes her and shakes her into responding. Again, all of a sudden, she reciprocates, and they're reconciled, and go down below together, to the ranting of le père Jules against lovers.

In *Zéro de conduite*, when one of the schoolboys in the dormitory gets up and walks in the night, another calls out not to disturb him as it might kill him. The somnambulistic gestures of Jean, in the seeming underworld of shades and fog, as he looks for Juliette in irrational fear that she has gone, evoke a comparable mood of anxiety, looking forward to the eventual, real disappearance of his love into the capital city he has forbidden her to enter. Distant echoes of mythic tropes stir: in classical and modern folklore, the prohibition sets the plot in motion. Here Jean forbids Juliette to discover 'Paris', a code word for the world available outside the barge, and in doing so returns to form as the husband-ogre, the Bluebeard who denies knowledge of the secret chamber and, while threatening to punish curiosity, still hands over the key to the door – just as Jean is making for Paris, for the docks at La Villette, and owns the radio which gives Juliette the news of the city's pleasures. He too lies under a prohibition, however, adumbrated by the test of the water. He must love his bride to be worthy of her, and love requires trust – until he achieves this he cannot hold her. When he gropes in the darkness to find her in the night of the fog, his fear implies his vulnerability in this area. Until he can dream her with his inner eye, he risks losing her from his sight in the real world.

Juliette's skirt and le père Jules

The heavy hand of morality lies on the love story in Jean Guinée's original script; as in a Victorian nursery version of Bluebeard, Juliette will learn to obey her husband. Jean Vigo's film not only draws the poisonous leadenness from the main structure of the narrative, but lights up all the corners of the script, too, playing his wit and high spirits over the bits in-between until they take on the character of cardinal points. *L'Atalante* would not be the original romance it is without le père Jules. Yet the old man does not make himself necessary to the plot in any material way until the conclusion. He is of himself a figure in-between, whose acts energise the erotic core of the film.

Two extraordinary sequences – The Skirt and The Cabinet of Curiosities – feature Michel Simon at his most effective. Throughout the film, he plays for all he's worth, clowning and mugging much as he did as the outcast *clochard* two years before in Jean Renoir's *Boudu sauvé des eaux*, but the tedious winsomeness of the boulevard comedy role has been sharpened with a touch of genuine menace, and the tramp's shambolic shagginess becomes genuinely ungainly. He also looks much older than he did as Boudu, and from this air of having lived he's able to develop crucial themes in the love story. Again, the action between Jean and Juliette takes place to the side, in the cabin of le père Jules, and what passes between the mate and Juliette is fraught with meaning, not for them, but for Jean. As the scene with the cat's new litter revealed, le père Jules represents a certain earthiness of response; but he's also threatening, in the eyes of Juliette and of the audience, with his rough, unceremonious gestures, his shabby, even grotesque appearance, his grumbling recalcitrance.

He is changed before our eyes in the course of the scene; a window opens not only on his character, but on possibilities beyond the barge – pleasures carnal and dreamlike. The nine shots of the skirt scene also show the team's control of shallow space, the dazzling cropping of figures in intimate contact – so that the action always spills, in the viewer's eye, beyond the frame – and their skill in capturing Simon's ebullient performance in long, single takes.

Inconsequentiality continually marks shifts of mood in *L'Atalante*, and the scene of the skirt, with all its madcap glints of wildness, takes place immediately after heavy umbrage has developed between le père Jules and Juliette at the table where they have been eating. She refuses to be ruffled by his sulking, and when he comes to stand beside her at the sewing machine, he seems to crawl through the door on account of his clumsy bulk. He gives the wheel a sharp blow to quicken its turning, and then again, in a gesture full of latent violence, as he edges right up to her on the seat to try a seam. She accepts his proximity without protest – the shot from behind of Simon's back and bottom slap up beside the slight

figure of Juliette in her silky spotted peignoir inspires a terrific
frisson in the viewer. The old ship's mate is firmly flouting the
distance between *la patronne* and himself which he had so heavily
ironised before, and in return Juliette compliments him with equal
irony on his prowess at sewing a seam like her. He boasts of many
other things he has done, and lifts both his hands to demonstrate
round her neck how he once strangled someone. 'In Shanghai,
during my time there,' he growls. Juliette shoves him and he falls
down, almost whining. Then, in one of the most delicious surprises
of the film, Juliette deflects the pretence assault and all the dangers it
carries in the minds of the audience, and orders him, as he knows so
much, to put on the skirt she's making so that she can pin the hem.

The invention is inspired: she's showing her irrepressible and
forgiving sense of life, which makes her such a sympathetic heroine;
she's keeping, in spite of his bogeyman antics, a cool-headed sense
of proportion, which also implies her secure self-possession and
knowledge that her body is her own, and can't be just taken so casually,

Le père Jules tries on the skirt

in play or in earnest. At the same time, she's also improvising on the theme close to Vigo's heart, which makes a strong showing in *Zéro de conduite*, for example: the limits of sexual categorisation. Juliette and le père Jules's first scene together points up, with a sense of fun, the folly of predetermined demarcations. You're such a tough guy, she is saying, but look, in a trice I can turn you into a woman! She's reminding him of his earlier parody of himself as a lackey emasculated by a new mistress; and le père Jules's fancy is now tickled by the masquerade. He makes a show of protesting, but she punches him in the tummy – catching the rawness of his own body language. Then Michel Simon grasps his moment and passes, in a quick series of sketches, excitedly citing place after place – 'Yokohama! Melbourne! Shanghai! Papeete! San Francisco!' – and slipping from one kind of music and music and movement to another, singing snatches of gibberish and first wiggling and writhing 'African'-style. 'Tu te crois encore chez les nègres, hein?' ('So you think you're still among the blacks, huh?') she says. The skirt turns him into a woman, then immediately into a native, a cipher where gender doesn't matter as generalised outsiderdom swallows up the distinctions – the skirt becomes a grass skirt or a witchdoctor's girdle – and Juliette, exclaiming at his swivelling hips that he must think he's back in Africa, pricks him with one of the pins she's using on the hem. He giggles, but he slaps the table like a drum, undeterred: 'Dorothy, 1903!' he boasts, then returns to his travels – 'Singapore! San Sebastian!' He begins flinging her skirt around like a matador, and Juliette snatches it back. He's irrepressible, and slides onto a chair to kick out his legs in a Russian dance.

In 1933, Vigo had considered adapting one of La Fouchardière's stories, *Clown par amour,* with the circus clown Béby in the role, and he must have chosen Simon for his gift at this kind of semi-grotesque comic turn. With the interest in authentic vulgarity also shown by the Surrealists, Vigo drew on the traditional, popular entertainment skills of the French, and liked all types of burlesque, vaudeville, conjuring and slapstick. Chaplin was one of his heroes, and he even contrived to meet him once, in Nice, though they could hardly address a word to each other.[16] Later in *L'Atalante*, the pedlar demonstrates clownish charm of the callow puppy variety, by contrast to Michel Simon's old sea-dog mastery. In *Zéro de conduite*, it's Jean Dasté as the new master Huguet who is given the clown part, who mimics Chaplin and silly-walks playing football in the school yard, like Max Linder.

A cut interrupts Michel Simon's Russian dance, and Juliette comes back into the cabin with his fresh laundry. Unpredictably, once again, the mood of the film has changed, and she's very cold with him. She orders him to go and join *le patron* and do some work. He complains, almost childishly, that he's tired, then questions, muttering aloud, who the *patron* is – the scene of intimacy with Juliette has altered the balance of their three-cornered relations.

The scene has been filled with odd, jostling moments of touching, all taking place in the cramped space; the fifth shot, over her left shoulder, out of focus as she works at the sewing machine, holds the emptiness of the bench beyond the small round table until Michel Simon walks into the gap. The table has a fringed, woven mat and a cut-glass stem fruit dish on it; the shelf behind is lined with a bobbled lace runner. These genteel surroundings set off the grotesque corporeality of le père Jules in his thin, ancient, patched *bleu de travail*; Michel Simon's elastic hips, his flexible wrists, his rubbery face and body, the feel of dirty, stubby rawness emanating from his presence, all keys up the sensual unease of the encounter.

When the boy calls out 'Paris!', Juliette emerges to see the city she was dreaming of before; still in her dressing gown, she climbs on deck. We see the men toiling at the lock gates, Jean heaving on the capstan, the boy hauling on the rope to pull the barge forward. These images of their work, its industrial, urban character, recall the social realism of contemporary photography, and it was probably fortunate that there wasn't enough money to film shots of Paris, of the Eiffel Tower and other sights, as planned, and that Vigo and Kaufman had to stick to the backwaters of the transport system, with its grainy, abstract aesthetic. The images honour such work, but without the heavy-handedness of Soviet films of the period.

Once again, however, Juliette's behaviour runs against audience expectations, as she puts her head out of the hatch. For when she realises that everyone is busy, she doesn't rush to dress and join them on land, but takes the opportunity to steal into le père Jules's quarters in the bows.

She's listening to a huge scallop shell in his cabin, when he comes through the door. 'Paris', the world of lights and fashion and excitement, has been displaced into the little world inside the barge in le père Jules's ambience. She may have been stern at the end of the skirt scene, but the mood has passed, and her curiosity, the dynamic of the heroine under a prohibition, is once more alight. Le père Jules can release her from the barge's constraints, open doors onto carnality, abundance, exoticism, imagination, excitement.

In the *Wunderkammer*

Rattles, tinkling musical boxes, a sawfish bone, hats from places faraway, Oriental lovelies lounging in posters, a fan, photographs, an elephant tusk and many of the mementos of le père Jules's former life crowd the tiny cabin he shares with the boy. As Juliette explores its contents and asks the old man about them, the camera works in closer and closer on them both until le père Jules eventually strips to show his tattoos. The dramatic movement of this, Juliette's second encounter alone with the old man, circles the paraphernalia of his room and gradually closes in tighter and tighter on the matter of his body. The representative of a kind of crudeness – of nature in the raw, as it were – he also stimulates imaginings of tropical pleasures and intense liaisons, of fun and laughter and music. He operates the pedals from behind the mechanical mannikin, and as the puppet with the wild hair and hollow eyes and ragged clothes jerks the baton like a demonic maestro, Juliette, with sparkling eyes, winds the chimes she's holding in response.

His talk becomes more personal, and the camera moves in tighter, until the moment when he picks up the knife and tells her it's a *navaja* – the kind of Spanish knife associated with macho feuds to the death, which the mother in Lorca's *Bodas de sangre*, for instance, will not have in her sight because such a weapon has killed her husband and her son.[17] To show her how sharp it is, the old man cuts his hand near the root of the thumb. There follows a tight close-up of Juliette – only the second such shot in the film – and she is sticking out the tip of her tongue. Just as when the cats scratched Jean's face Juliette relented, so now she's attracted. Her tongue quivers, in and out, twice, as le père Jules licks the blood he has drawn.

After this appearance of a darker brand of eroticism than the cuddling of Jean has aroused hitherto, Juliette continues to prowl through the goodies in the old sailor's Pandora's box; she finds a photograph of a young man, standing half-dressed between two South Sea beauties. She reads the image as a picture of le père Jules – not the shambling, grizzled and prognathous workman beside her but a slim and smiling youth. Then, when she opens a cupboard, and for once the camera does lift the wall in order to watch her reaction

Juliette and the severed hands

from the other side, she sees a jar containing a pair of severed hands. She gasps; but matters of the body have been granted such a valued place that even this gruesome collectible does not shock her deeply. Le père Jules explains that the hands are all that's left to him of his friend ('C'est tout ce qui me reste de lui'). A life of intimacies, and the implication of deep, close friendship, regardless of sex, reverberate under this simple sentence of regret. The image connects, more remotely, with le père Jules's piratical character: pirates were legendary for their male camaraderie, their contracts of *compagnonnage* which would will one boon companion to another after death. The remark, following so closely on the handsome photograph of le père Jules's friend and the sight of his grisly keepsake, undoubtedly carries homoerotic overtones, placed in the film to hint at forbidden passions and to introduce perhaps an idea of their naturalness. Immediately after this exchange, le père Jules uncovers his tattooed body. His actions are playful – he jokes that tattoos keep him warm, then sticks a cigarette in his navel where a

Jules's tattooed torso

woman's mouth has been painted. (This shot disappeared from the cut shown in 1934 and for a long time was known only from a still.)

Though the mood of his display is shyly mischievous and certainly not enticing or seductive, the tattoos convey the marks of history – the marks of story – on the old man's body. Among the usual pin-ups, the initials MAV appear – for the nineteenth-century battlecry, later adapted by the anarchists: Mort aux Vaches (Death to the Pigs).[18] By contrast, Juliette's past is a tabula rasa and her longing for experience – to be marked – is roused by the testimony of his room, his curiosities; his fantasy, his written-on body. Drawn to him, where he now sits, on the lower bunk playing a tarantella on the accordion (in fact the 'Chanson des mariniers'), she begins to comb his hair. Above him, the shot wittily includes a giant comb of a sawfish's blade with its widely set tines. Michel Simon puts eloquent, giggling pleasure into his remark. 'Je ne suis pas habitué a des douceurs' ('I'm not used to kindnesses'). When Jean bursts in on this intimate ritual, the cats return to play their crucial part. 'It's poisonous in here,' shouts Jean in his fury, hurling a cat out of the way. 'The filth,' he cries. Cat, as in English 'pussy', has sexual connotations – later, the *camelot* will joke about biscuits 'archisèches comme la chatte de l'archi-duchesse' ('super-dry like the arch-duchess's pussy'). To emphasise Jean's allusion, the camera cuts to a rare close-up, an image in-between, of a completely naked black girl.

The Orientalist theme of sexy exotic otherness runs strongly through film of the 1930s: *Marius*, for instance, directed by Alexander Korda in 1931 and produced by Marcel Pagnol from his own novel, dramatises the lure of the French Caribbean for Marius, who works in his father's cafe on the quay of the Old Harbour in Marseilles. Two years later came *King Kong*, one of the most horrific of Orientalist views of the exotic; the bric-a-brac in le père Jules's cabin, with its strong flavour of foreign, even freakish marvels and its attraction for the freedom they seem to flourish before the viewer's eyes, belongs in the same mindset as *King Kong*. Vigo himself played an enthusiastic part in furnishing le père Jules's

cabin, gathering stuff from several scrap and flea markets, as well as from friends. The film's still photographer, Roger Parry, provided the South Sea island material, brought back from a trip to Tahiti the year before. Vigo was himself interested in travelling far afield, and had proposed, to Nounez, that they film one of his scripts, *Le Bagne* (*The Prison Colony*), in French Guiana.

Immediately after the close-up on the photograph of the naked girl, Juliette, the unpredictable Juliette, who is proving such a quick pupil at carnal insouciance and pleasure in the ambience of le père Jules, does not behave as the heroines of fairy tales usually do and weep at her fate; she collapses laughing out of sheer high spirits on le père Jules's bunk. An incomprehensible shot follows, from the other side of the bed, showing the old man lifting himself away from her as she lies there; a cat jumps out again too. Jean then pulls her to her feet and hits her. He begins to smash things – the fight proceeds awkwardly, convincingly, with none of the expressionist overkill in Renoir's *La Fille de l'eau* (1925) for instance, of a decade before.

Among le père Jules's souvenirs …

Vigo's direction resists rhetoric – he keeps the gestures few and meaningful and ungainly. But a black cat leaps across in flight and a sudden montage of close-ups shows the broken bric-a-brac in the cabin as well as the cat's fright, the knife Jean has thrown in anger which has pierced the floor. Then le père Jules comes back into the room. He has had his hair cropped close to his scalp, by a dog-trimmer on the quay.

There's no *gueule* in the movies like Michel Simon's – except perhaps for Fernandel's, and he used it only for comic effect – and this close-up of his great mug, the single example in *L'Atalante*, is charged with wry pathos. The old man, in his ugliness, which the brutal crop underlines, has expiated in the traditional penitential act of hair-cutting his daring to be physical, to bring his body into the story, with its memories of pleasures and even its capacity to start up new dreams of the same.

Back in her own cabin, Juliette looks at herself in the mirror and ruffles her own hair. She is inspecting herself for change, for

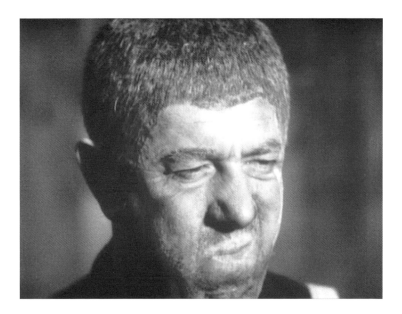

Michel Simon as Jules, shorn

renewed expectations, for changing feelings; meanwhile le père Jules picks up the jagged shards of the mirror in which she was partially reflected while combing his matted hair, and which Jean has broken. 'Sept ans de malheur,' he comments – his superstitiousness (the horseshoes) forms a consistent background theme, and relates to his concluding role as a kind of magician who sets all to rights. But at this point the climate of anxiety returns, and Jean fears – for the third time – that Juliette has disappeared. And in a way – the way of imagination – she has.

The plot never holds the centre of the director's attention; the changing colours of behaviour do, and the performances rise to the challenge, giving unusual subtlety and range to the characters on board 'L'Atalante'. Vigo himself once expressed himself vehemently on the subject of others' unknowability, and the imprisonment of narcissism: 'D'un être, autant que l'on désire le comprendre il faut, je crois, renoncer à atteindre jamais sa réalité … Quelle angoisse ne ressent-on pas à cette course devant le labyrinthe de glaces, qui nous livrent que l'image de notre image, et toujours, de notre image?'[19]

Vigo and Surrealism

The Cabinet of Curiosities scene exemplifies several Surrealist precepts, as we shall see, but above all it affirms the power and value of imagination. André Breton, in his autobiographical novels *Nadja* (1928) and *L'Amour fou* (1931), had uncovered 'le merveilleux' he sought in the prosaic and daily comings and goings of urban life. Nadja, the muse and love object who can open the key to mysteries, materialises almost by magic in the street, and Breton follows her through flea markets, cafes, cheap hotels, illustrating his odyssey with photographs by Man Ray and Jacques-André Boiffard of sites and omens and the general 'fury of symbols' he finds in the 'legible city'. Vigo agreed that 'l'insolite est quotidien' ('The unusual is mundane')[20] and, in a similar manner to Breton, he scatters portents and hunches and odd, everyday miracles into the narrative of *L'Atalante*. Automata are almost a signature of Surrealism.

The journal *Minotaure*, in December 1933 while Vigo was shooting, published an issue with several articles on puppets: Benjamin Péret's 'Au Paradis des fantômes' reflected on clocks, watches, guns with singing birds, musical monkeys and a mechanical 'writer', in a rather uncanny echo of le père Jules's cabin.[21] Vigo also wanted to seize the deeper meaning of the world of appearances and read random gesture or coincidence for its hidden import – Breton's *hasard objectif*; objective chance, which can yield up truths all unconsciously. Vigo said,

Le but sera atteint si l'on parvient à réveler la raison cachée d'un geste, à extraire d'une personne banale et de hasard sa beauté intérieure ou sa caricature ... Et cela avec une force telle que désormais le monde qu'autrefois nous côtoyions avec indifférence s'offre à nous malgré lui, au-delà de ses apparences.[22]

This ambition, itself true to Surrealist first principles, found one of its most expressive instruments in the image of a woman; Jean's Orpheus-like pursuit and loss of Juliette even recalls Breton's relation to Nadja in his book, and the central, magical, erotic power of Juliette in Vigo's film also represents the Surrealists' vision of woman, at that precise historical moment.

Breton's second Surrealist manifesto was published in 1930, his third would appear the same year as *L'Atalante*. The interconnections were close: Roger Parry, who worked on the stills of *L'Atalante*, had been directly influenced by the example of *Nadja* to illustrate a novel with photographs; significantly, it was called *Banalités* (1930).[23] But whereas Breton, a true modernist surgeon questioning a distempered part, strikes a cerebral, disconnected note, Vigo's curiosity bubbles warmly. Though he was a passionate admirer of *Un Chien andalou* (1929), introducing a showing of his own first film, *À propos de Nice*, with a eulogy of Dali and Buñuel, he never emulated their provocative callousness. Indeed, so soft was Vigo that he eliminated certain moments from *Zéro de conduite* –

scenes of bullying, for instance, and an insulting remark about the children made by the guard at the station. Dali and Buñuel's world of enchantment and rebellion was made of much sterner stuff. Vigo is perhaps the only film-maker, writes Gilles Jacob, to have created 'tin merveilleux intimiste' ('a marvellousness of intimacy').[24]

His ability to fuse the marvellous with the quotidian helps Vigo's surrealism to avoid the clunking contrivance of some of the movement's cinematic symbolism, like *La Coquille et le clergyman* (*The Seashell and the Clergyman*), which Germaine Dulac, later Vigo's patron, directed in 1928 from a script by Antonin Artaud (though Artaud dissociated himself in fury from the results). In *Zéro de conduite*, Vigo had included an elliptical scene of classic Surrealist titillation, when Caussat goes home to his guardian at the weekend and plays, blindfolded, with his little white-knickered daughter.

In *L'Atalante*, Vigo has put such quotations behind him, and is able to give the portrait of Juliette an individuality most Surrealist images of women do not even attempt. Dita Parlo is a *femme-enfant*, but her inner world matters more even than her outer appeal. She is, as James Agee noted, 'the fullest embodiment of sub-articulate sex that I have seen'. In his perceptive eulogy of *L'Atalante*, Agee then went on to point to a most telling association: 'Michel Simon, as a pre-mental old man, is even more wonderfully realized as a poetic figure, a twentieth-century Caliban.'[25] Agee puts his finger here on Dita Parlo's childishness, her Miranda-like qualities of discovery and innocence and acceptance.

The proportions of Dita Parlo's features and limbs accentuate the atmosphere, inside the cabinet of curiosities, that a *femme-enfant*, someone young and untried, is being awakened by someone old and tried. Her very high wide forehead gives her face a bright candour, and the four tiny wrinkles that form when she expresses sadness or disappointment appear far up near the hairline, as in a child's face rather than, as in an adult's, between the eyebrows. She has also the wide-set eyes of a girl, while the slenderness of her torso and her hips shows through the simple clothes she wears. It was 1933–4, after all, when stars of other films about love are wearing slinky numbers with

Juliette leaning on the tiller in her glowing wedding dress, the blank sky, the silhouetted hulk of industrial works on the banks, and the delicate reflection of her feet: this still exemplifies Vigo's aesthetic in *L'Atalante*

décolletage and trussed contours. Juliette's clothes are by contrast unglamorous and modest, faithful to the thrifty milieu of a working barge, and her underwear doesn't mould her body into sexy definition. When she dresses up, she looks as if she intends to be smart and pretty, not seductive; she doesn't wear make-up that can be seen, and putting on her garters in the cabin, she merely slips them on under her dress without lingering on the task to look at her legs or the camera fetishising her action. When she comes up on deck to help Jean move the drunken père Jules down below and he hoots, 'La patronne en chemise!' ('The missus in her nightie!'), it's noteworthy that this garment is a floor-length, voluminous white shirt which reveals nothing.

As an innocent discovering erotic desire, Dita Parlo's Juliette embodies radiantly the *femme-enfant* idealised by André Breton and the movement, the innocent vehicle through whom men could reach greater knowledge, more intense pleasure. She fulfils the definition of 'La Femme' proposed in *Le Dictionnaire abrégé du surréalisme*, in which Breton paraphrased Baudelaire: 'La Femme est l'être qui projète la plus grande ombre ou la plus grande lumière dans nos rêves.'[26] But in Vigo's film she also takes the role further: we are interested in her dreams too, not only our own about her. Her presence opens a window onto a benign realm of tenderness and pleasure, not a site of discipline, travail or cruelty – of erotic power as it appears more usually in both Surrealism and contemporary film portraits of seductive females.

The theme of innocence relates *L'Atalante* closely to *Zéro de conduite*, a dissimilar film in almost every other way. Both make passionate statements about personal and emotional freedom and the expression of individual preferences and desires with an anarchic, antinomian *joie de vivre* which can also be found in some of the best self-declared Surrealist image-making. In *Zéro de conduite*, the plotline hinges on the teacher's prurient suspicions about the friendship between Bruel, a large mischief-maker, and Tabard, the new boy with delicate features, long hair and short tunics, who's so homesick he goes home for one more night with his mother. He's nothing but 'une fille' (subtitled 'sissy') protests Caussat, the leading member of the gang when his friend, Colin, wants to let Tabard join them. But Tabard proves his mettle. He has been told by the dwarfish headmaster that his friendship with Bruel is unwholesome; he's visibly upset when he returns to the classroom, and then swears at the teacher who tries to comfort him by placing his huge fat hand over the boy's. When asked to apologise in front of the headmaster and his deputation, he repeats his insult: 'Je vous dis merde!' ('Fuck you!'). The reply triggers the boys' revolution against their masters – the ecstatic pillowfight and nocturnal procession in the dorm and the manic disruption of the school's anniversary celebrations the next day. With regard to *L'Atalante*, *Zéro de conduite*'s attack on authority becomes especially fascinating because it's Tabard, the girlish and frail new boy, who emerges as the most uncompromising madcap rebel leader of them all.

Vigo's biographer P. E. Salles Gomes comments that just as Vigo can be recognised in Tabard in *Zéro de conduite* for obvious reasons (see below), so, in *L'Atalante*, he identifies with Juliette. Vigo's anarchic, adversarial relation to received ideas made him rebel against first principles of sexual ascription: to him the sissy could be a hero, and boys could be intimate friends. In *L'Atalante*, he defied received ideas with equal *désinvolture* – the husband who wants to exercise his authority over his wife's fantasy and erotic awakening gets no sympathy from him at all. Jean, when he smashes le père Jules's cabin, is acting like one of the petty-minded, joyless masters in a boarding school, seeing dirt in innocence, denying the variations possible on the theme of love and kinship. In this, Vigo and Riéra's interpretation of Guinée's script runs counter to everything it held dear: in Guinée, Jean has to achieve control of Juliette's waywardness in order to be a proper man. In Vigo, it's precisely le père Jules's rich affective life and Juliette's wonderful, generous capacity for pleasure which Jean isn't yet sufficiently awake to understand, caught as he still is in preconceptions about authority and obedience. But at the same time, Vigo isn't himself didactic – and the audience, tense from the ambiguities of le père Jules and Juliette's encounter, feels sympathy with Jean's fury.

The pedlar

Later that evening, the old man prevents the couple going out together by leaving the barge himself; Juliette, disappointed, becomes tetchy. During the mate's prolonged absence, Jean turns in bed and finds Juliette gone. He experiences his third terrified premonition that Juliette has vanished from his life. Jean Dasté stirs compassion in the audience with the sincerity of the terror he conveys to Juliette when he finds her back in bed and hugs her close. In fact she had gone above, and witnessed the return of le père Jules, roaring drunk, with a stolen horn for his gramophone. She leaves him to stumble aboard – he falls headlong down the ladder – and says nothing of it to Jean, even when Jean himself is roused by the noise.

Inconsequentiality, severing one event from another, throws into relief once again the volatile enigma of her nature. Together they heave the drunken père Jules onto his bunk – he continues to sing out, 'O Paris, O ville infâme et merveilleuse!' It was a popular song of the time, and however ironically we in the audience receive his rendition, it keeps in the foreground the theme of the city as lure, as sin, 'infamous, marvellous – amorous – Paris'.

The scene contains a glaring continuity error, because when they hump le père Jules down below, the gramophone horn lies on his bunk already. Salles Gomes explains that the mistake arises from a lengthy cut. The sequence has been lost, but it showed a major row developing between le père Jules and Jean, in which the old man goes to his cabin and fetches his revolver; he threatens Jean with it, but then shoots himself, making a hole in his trousers but not doing any more serious damage.

The episode would have added aggression to the texture of *L'Atalante*, and it would have swung more sympathy in Jean's direction. Even though Michel Simon's performance colours the film so vividly, a great deal more of the part, besides the revolver episode, was cut which gave le père Jules's character a sharply comic, absurd turn. In one sequence in Vigo's script, for instance, le père Jules, the boy, and the comic scrap dealer Raspoutine go shop-lifting in an Arab grocery; but while they're busy stealing oranges, the shopkeeper keeps filching things from le père Jules's bag. It's easy to see that such a piece of cynical comedy would have brought *L'Atalante* closer in mood to *L'Age d'or* (1930) and weakened the feeling of hopefulness and innocence typical of Vigo's films.[27]

Soon after this – maybe even the following night – Jean and Juliette leave the industrial jumble of the quayside and, arm in arm, Jean swinging along and capering in fine fettle, they arrive at a popular *estaminet*, 'Aux Quatre Saisons', festively decorated with coloured streamers (no doubt) and the Chinese paper lanterns which played such an effective part in the joyous dorm riot in *Zéro de conduite*. For the interior, the most elaborate set built for the film, the designer Francis Jourdain recreated a dance hall he remembered from his youth, with an inner, slightly lower pit caged in trellis; it's an odd, compressed stage, a fitting successor to the barge.

The *camelot* first appears on the docks, whirling down the embankment on his bicycle with a trunk strapped to the back. It bears the inscription, 'La volaille est à l'intérieue' ('The goods [literally, the fowl] are inside'). He nearly collides with Jean and Juliette, and scatters them, in a presage of his effect later. There's a sexy overtone also to his slangy graffiti, as well as the humorous, Surrealist connotations of the man-machine, the modern centaur. When we see the *camelot*'s bike later, parked against a vitrine near the entrance to the bar, his message seems to hint at excitements inside; at this stage, Jean and Juliette react gaily to this promise. When they walk in, the *camelot* is strumming a guitar, in a higgledy-piggledy heap of goods from his trunk. He's wearing a bowler hat and draped like a fool in motley with the fripperies he's peddling. He's breezy, slick, familiar, while his patter belongs to a uniquely Gallic genre of tongue-twister called a *contrepéterie* (counterfarts) full of alliteration and innuendo. Juliette, as to be expected by now, responds to his off-colour sallies with sparkling eyes. He conjures some doves for her before whirling off to do card tricks at another couple's table.

Gilles Margaritis's performance as the *camelot* draws on all the exuberance and energy of popular entertainment, of the boulevards, of vaudeville, of caf'conc singing. He adds light and wit and fun and caddish dazzle to the already rich mix of moods in *L'Atalante*, and rising up so vigorously and so animatedly into the middle of the movie, he springs a surprise that rounds out the film's patterns of enchantment. The audience cannot resist this genie peddling pleasure any more than Juliette can; in terms of the fairy-tale structure, he functions as the adversary, a wily seducer who must be resisted if the lovers are to flourish.

Charles Goldblatt, a journalist friend who met Vigo at the first showing of *À propos de Nice* in Paris and subsequently published a praising review, wrote the words for the pedlar's song, as he had also done for the 'Chanson des mariniers', and both use a dashing argot. The comical puns and rhymes advertising household wares as well as fantastic things, mixing up antiseptics and press-studs, stainless steel knives and Adam's apples, are wittily underlined by Maurice Jaubert's music so that the couplets trip along with contagious vitality:

Des chateaux d'cart' pour vos enfants
Des ch'veux à r'vendre et des cur'dents …
(Houses of cards for your kids,
Recycled hair and toothpicks.)[28]

The impishness of the list matches the dancing eyes and smiles of Gilles Margaritis as he flirts so outrageously with Juliette. It would have been so much more expected to have him sing a love song, but the jauntiness of this completely irrelevant chatter about novelties from Paris works as an invitation to love far more potent than any moonlight serenade.

The *patron* of 'Aux Quatre Saisons' loses patience with the pedlar; tumult breaks out on the floor as the dancers invade it and he tries to gather up his goods. But as Juliette watches, anxious on his behalf, he still snatches the chance to coquette with her, using a monkey glove puppet, and then dances over to sell her a scarf. Jean pays for it, and the *camelot* suddenly lifts Juliette bodily through one of the apertures in the trellis, claiming a dance with her as part payment; in his bumfreezer jacket, perkily sticking out his bottom to the rhythms of the java that Jaubert wrote for the dance scene, he holds her familiarly, promiscuously.[29] Other couples jig around them; later, a woman dancing with a black soldier playfully puts a tray on her head, parodying preconceptions of 'natives'. The box in which they are pressed close carries Juliette far beyond the sombre *rives* seen from Jean's barge.

Vigo cuts to a close-up of Jean at the table, smoking for the first time in the film, in a fury of jealousy. In the brawl that follows, after Jean angrily pushes the pedlar out of the way, Margaritis springs one more wonderful surprise: as the *patron* advances to throw him out, he does a dead man's drop on to his back before the man can reach him. It's one of those moments of invention which enrich *L'Atalante* throughout, and are never dwelt on. Though it's just a clown's piece of slapstick, it does reflect Vigo's love of interrupting the boring predictability of causal links in narrative. The victim falls before he's assaulted, just as illogically as Juliette's moods come and go and the wedding guests behave like funeral mourners.

Jean Guinée, in his synopsis, had introduced a sailor in love with Juliette, as indeed Puccini had done in *Il tabarro*; but his full script had changed the character to a pedlar from Paris, giving Vigo the idea which he developed so richly. When the *camelot* next appears, he has taken on the persona of another circus figure, the one-man band, a fantastical apparition which anticipates Fellini; with bells on his legs and ankles, a drum on his back, cymbals and trombone, he appears from the back, his trombone first, running into shot down the ramp to the canal walk. He lines himself up like a regimental drummer and starts marching forward, summoning Juliette on deck; again with smiling, devilish charm, he describes, in rap-like rhymes, the thrills of the capital, which lies so tantalisingly close by the docks of La Villette:

Une ville qui pète le feu. La ville lumière à tous les étages ...
Des vélos; des motos, des autos à capots pour Toto Parigot.
C'est beau!
Les Champs-Elysées pour Bébé. Les Tuileries pour Bibi. Notre-Dame
pour Madame ...[30]

Jean suddenly reappears behind him and boots him onto the quay; he scurries off, across the wide desolate wasteground round the docks with smoking chimneys and telegraph poles. This shot looks forward to the Pasolini of *Uccellacci e uccellini* (1966) and to Antonioni's urban deserts. The use of space throughout *L'Atalante* is telling; contrasting the compactness of the barge interiors and the dance-hall floor with the empty expanses of the fields round Juliette's village, with this industrial landscape and later the beach at Le Havre, Vigo sets up a tremendous feeling of disorientation. The *camelot* scampers off – who knows where? The plunging depth of field again accelerates the speed with which he disappears into the grim horizon, as the bells on his costume go on tinkling long after.

In bed that night, his invitation, too, continues to whisper in Juliette's ear, as well as Jean's anger. When Jean stops pacing up and down the deck and comes in to her, we do not see his face, but she turns away into the pillow in bitter reproach at what she sees there – a moment of acute psychological perception about quarrels. So she does play truant for real, crossing the bleak wasteland round the docks to find the station where the local train called the 'Tortillard' (the twister) will take her to the centre of Paris.

The city of modern life

When the fairy castle vanishes because the heroine has broken the prohibition, she often has to fight and struggle with hardship and other ordeals in order to regain her love. Psyche, for instance, in the founding fairy tale, disobeys Cupid's command that she must never look at him in the night and lights a lamp; a drop of the hot oil falls on his shoulder and wakes him up, whereupon everything vanishes – Cupid, his castle and all his enchantments – and Psyche finds herself alone, stranded. She's then put to appalling tasks and impossible trials by her mother-in-law Venus, and only when she has proved her love does the goddess of love relent and allow her to be reunited with Cupid again. After Juliette has spent a day in Paris, defying all Jean's directives, and returns to the docks, she finds that the barge has left and she's alone. It would be silly to suggest that any of the contributors to *L'Atalante* had the allegorical myth consciously in mind, but it would be also ignorant to dismiss the parallels for this reason. Enforced separation, usually blameless but sometimes less so, functions as a great spur to true love in the romance genre; it is simply one of the most available and efficient plot dynamics available.

Vigo finds an image to convey this fracture in the lovers' story – no words, only a shot of their empty bed, one of the most sensuous still lifes in the film, of softly gleaming pillows and rumpled bedclothes. We see Jean's face, the image of the bed returns, and Jean gives the order to leave, immediately, as the *patronn* has gone.

Jean Dasté's acting has been subdued till this point in the film, with none of the heightened theatricality of his performance as the schoolmaster in *Zéro de conduite*. But after Juliette has left for Paris, he infuses Jean with keyed-up, half-crazed despair. What he feared has come about – her disappearance – and his abandonment of her, spurred on by jealousy and hurt pride, produces a kind of catalepsy in him – *amour fou* in its dark mode. Dasté introduces small precise observations: in the midst of acting the boss with le père Jules, who protests that they should wait for Juliette to come back, Jean blows his nose with his hand. Vigo struggled with him, Dasté remembered later, to forget the theatre, and make his interpretation simple and direct.[31]

The automatic doors of the train close on a bewildered Juliette.

The metropolis she first discovers belongs to the Surrealists' private kingdom of desire; but when she finds herself stranded, Vigo draws more on realist and expressionist styles. Photography had been the profession of Vigo's step-grandfather, with whom he was brought up for a while, and knowledge of the medium, both still and moving, shows clearly in Boris Kaufman and Vigo's *À propos de Nice*, of three years before, which evokes the Riviera town with detailed attention to contrast, angle, visual rhymes and surprises, somewhat in the manner of 'city films' of the 1920s, like René Clair's *Paris qui dort* (1924), and Dziga-Vertov's *Man with a Movie Camera* (1929). In the section on Paris in *L'Atalante*, Vigo shows his social concerns with the poverty and unemployment of the 1930s, while Kaufman produces sombre lighting and deep angular shadows for the setting of the almost entirely silent action. Dziga-Vertov's surname was Kaufman, and Boris Kaufman always said that they were in fact brothers. So it is possible that the films are connected not only by

À propos de Nice (1930)

iconography and attitude, but by family relationship too. However, Kaufman does not seem to have worked in Russia or with Vertov, and the lines of influence are hard to draw.[32]

With time pressing, and the late season of the year, the scenes in Paris let no sunshine in – unlike the harsh sunlight of *À propos de Nice*. *L'Atalante* predominantly takes place in a bluesy shadowland, and when Juliette discovers Paris it is the city promised by the *camelot* in one way, a city of artificial light on every floor, a nocturnal place where outdoors has an indoor quality. On her truant afternoon, to the jaunty fairground accompaniment of the *camelot*'s ballad on cymbals and barrel-organ, Juliette gazes at windows full of jewels and fashions; she then stops before a *tableau vivant* of Parisian strollers and visitors, pictured as out in the streets, taking the air, though they are in fact lifelessly displayed under glass. With their Atget-influenced doubled reflections and the eerie life-in-death quality of simulacra, these costumed automata in the vitrine only adumbrate the sinister aspects of metropolitan pleasures, the tendency to grotesque excess of the urban rich, like the carnival giants in *À propos de Nice*. The window cleverly compresses the ideas of cosmopolitanism and dalliance Juliette was expected to find in Paris, and shows them to be false – puppets, illusions.

For, after she finds that the barge has sailed away, the cheery music of the new leisure stops, and the city bares its teeth.

At the station, Juliette is eyed by a vulpine, emaciated man; when she gets out her purse to pay for her ticket, he snatches it. In a crowd scene filmed from above, as harsh as in a Fritz Lang film, the bystanders chase him, catch him and beat him to the ground. While she watches, aghast, another leering, half-idiot man with a stick jostles her; then, in a long panning shot, under Juliette's eyes, the thief's limp body is dragged, his face stunned and bleeding, behind a long railing into the custody of two policemen. Nobody gives her any comfort; she's now penniless as well as alone. Silently and harrowingly, the camera follows her shifting emotions, from her

Eugène Atget, 'Avenue des Gobelins' (1925)

first fear and horror of the starving thief to dismay at the crowd's
enthusiastic assault on him and pity for his imprisonment – marked
by the long line of bars along which he's dragged. After this, Juliette
continues to wander; she's accosted by men, she's turned away from
jobs, she drifts down industrial side streets outside factories where
men stand in line hoping for work. She becomes one of the mass of
the urban poor in the 1930s – Vigo and Kaufman used an actual job
seekers' queue to film this section. They keep the camera at a
distance from her, not only because on land they can draw away to
show her full-length, but also to point up her vulnerability and
anonymity in the crowd. The only close-up shows her feet, trudging
along in dirty snow from a distant point right up to the camera.

Though many of these pitfalls reflect conventional warnings
to young women against city life, Vigo manages to root Juliette's
disillusionment in her feelings for Jean, rather than wag a finger at
a girl for straying. He avoids sentimentality, by reintroducing

'Down industrial side streets ...'

ironically upbeat accordion music on the soundtrack. But he does not have a chance, given the romance he is telling, to counter with his usual anarchic contrariness the prevailing moral arguments about the dangers for women. These have been shown, in studies like Elizabeth Wilson's *The Sphinx in the City* (1991) and Judith Walkowitz's *City of Dreadful Delight* (1992), to lie as much in male anxiety about the freedom cities and work could offer women as in the actual hazards that faced them. Nevertheless, for Juliette, the Paris which the *camelot* had conjured turns out to be a lie, its existence possible only in fantasy. It's significant, however, that Vigo does not point an accusing finger at Juliette. In Guinée's script, she spends all her money on frivolities, and the story clearly intends her to stand as a warning to giddy girls who would behave like her given half a chance.

The barge, by contrast to the city, now takes on the character of a magical space of safety and dreaming, and the events taking place there during Juliette's absence reinforce this: Jean, in semi-catatonic state of hollow-eyed despair, plays chequers with le père Jules, oblivious to the old man's arrant cheating. Abruptly, he plunges his head inside a bucket, trying to summon Juliette's image. When, still stricken dumb, he leaves the cabin, Michel Simon picks up the record, thinking that if they can get the gramophone to play, they might be able to cheer him up. He runs his finger along the grooves, and music sounds; he tries again, the same thing happens: the haunting tune first heard over the couple on their way to the barge from the church plays under his hand. He stops and the music carries on – the boy has been accompanying his action on the accordion. But this ruse turns out to have melted the bad magic holding the barge in thrall, for le père Jules finds, when he puts the record on the turntable, that the machine is suddenly working.

On board, Jean, looking once again like a sleepwalker, dives into the grey water of the canal; it's the start of the most extraordinary scene of enchantment in the whole of *L'Atalante*. The camera keeps close to him as he searches for Juliette with open eyes.

Jean underwater; the vision of Juliette

He swims about, making the realistically effortful strokes of a man underwater, and the camera catches his ungainliness in what look like turbid depths; bubbles stream from him as he swims into view upside down, then somersaults and goes on searching, horizontal to the screen.

Vigo had been commissioned to make a short film, in 1930, about the champion swimmer Taris, and he had been attracted to it because he could film the athlete through the portholes of a pool where he exercised.[33] In *Taris: roi de l'eau*, Vigo added touches of his characteristic humour and invention – at the end of the film the swimmer flips straight out of the water on to the side in reverse motion and then walks across its surface. In *L'Atalante*, Vigo didn't use this kind of Méliès-like trick, but conjured deeper dream magic out of the water imagery. Suddenly, as anyone who has ever seen the film will never forget, Juliette appears suspended, superimposed in front of Jean's eyes, in her wedding dress, in flight, turning round slowly to face out towards us. The image dissolves into Jean's flattened, straining face in distorted close-up – Vigo had commented that he liked the way the pressure affected Taris's features – and then dissolves again to Juliette in close-up. Dita Parlo's smile here, as her eyes, her mouth, her cheeks, her hair under her bridal wreath light up, must count as simply one of the most dazzling images of a loving woman in the history of cinema. Many film-makers have tried to come near its erotic radiance – some of Godard's close-ups of Anna Karina, and the last shot of Claudia Cardinale in Fellini's *8½* (1963), approach it – but Dita Parlo's smile holds the screen with unique joy.

When Jean emerges, his catatonia has deepened; the boy and le père Jules decide to bring him the gramophone, now miraculously repaired, to play to him. The shot of them walking along the bows of the barge hauntingly rhymes the trumpet of the horn with the sunhat the boy has borrowed from le père Jules's cabinet, in a tiny Vigo-style procession of pleasure and freedom. But even this cannot unlock Jean's autistic silence. In the cabin, when they put the

gramophone down, all the cats crawl towards the sound, one even investigating the trumpet and settling down in it. Vigo had not set up this wonderful shot, but was delighted of course when the six cats spontaneously assumed their parts, for their presence confirms the return of possibilities – of love and intimacy and joy and carnality. The boy and the old man try to rouse Jean, drying him and dressing him, but to no avail. There's an abrupt cutaway at this point, a section of film restored to the 1990 version, showing Jean with his arms wrapped around a huge block of ice, rubbing his cheeks on it, licking and fondling it.

When the lovers go to bed in their separate rooms that night, Vigo and/or his editor Louis Chavance create an astonishing montage, which builds on the erotic promise of Jean's vision. In a series of dissolves, we see Jean and Juliette tossing in longing for each other, their hands and even their mouths caressing themselves

Jean embraces the block of ice

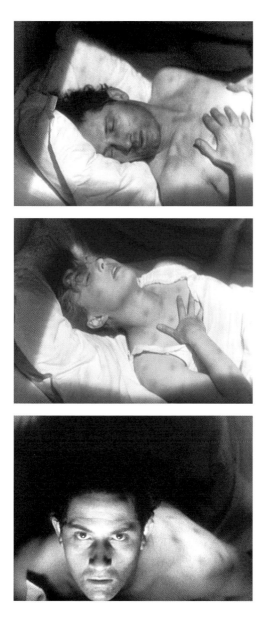

The lovers in their separate rooms

as they dream of the other. The images imply the physical more than show it, however – these are not sequences of filmed masturbation, but of sheets moving, pillows dipping under heavy heads. The images of both are taken through a spotted filter – the frosted glass of their cabin door on the barge? – but the effect recalls drops of water and brings back the test Jean has now passed. The camera comes in closer on their faces than ever before, for the first time showing them together with such intimacy (their earlier cuddling and kissing took place mostly in half-length shots). In the climax, which is not orgiastically satisfactory in the strenuous present-day style, the editing merges them into each other: as the slow motion recalls the somnambulist effortfulness of swimming, and develops the motif of the earlier vision underwater, Jean's head comes up to face outwards in close-up in the attitude of searching; as it drops down again it fades into Juliette's shadow and her face enters the screen, eyes open as she tosses in her longing. All the while, Jaubert's wedding waltz is being played on that melancholy alto sax.

Love regained

The working conditions of Jean and his crew rumble intermittently in the deep background of the film – he's anxious to make up time at the start, and when they reach Le Havre the film's iconographic subtext – its 'poem to working-class individuals' existence', in Sally Potter's phrase[34] – inspires a grainy montage of cranes and derricks, woodyards, ferries, steam trains, buckets and pulleys as their cargo is unloaded. Lucid storytelling was never one of Vigo's main concerns – in *Zéro de conduite* there are many loose ends and several highly compressed and unintelligible moments – and in *L'Atalante* he similarly pays rather cursory attention to the plot.

When Jean's despair at his separation from Juliette deepens at Le Havre, he begins to behave strangely onshore as well as on the barge, running out along the breakwater and climbing down a quayside ladder and then plunging across the empty beach towards a liner as if Juliette might be on board. He seems to disappear

towards the vanishing point much faster than any man could run; Bill Brandt in his photography of beaches twenty years later would use a similar formal device to produce an atmosphere of unease.

When Jean returns, staggering, to the quay, le père Jules and the boy rescue him from the unpleasant attention of several 'bosses'; they have taken him for 'another drunken sailor'. (The image of him licking ice would fit better here, where the iceblocks could plausibly be standing on the quayside for loading.) His behaviour comes to the notice of the barge company, and at Le Havre, Jean is summoned to explain himself. The mate takes charge of the interview with the peremptory, disagreeable manager, and when informed that there have been complaints against the skipper of 'L'Atalante', he sticks up for Jean and saves the situation. The stress of the scene falls on the uncouthness of the white-collar employee and the gallantry of the worker, the old man, in protecting his younger captain; in this respect, Vigo's loyalties run counter to current contempt for manual

Jean runs across the beach

labour, as evinced even in film-makers like Jean Renoir.[35] In *La Fille de l'eau*, for instance, the bargee-uncle of the heroine, Virginie, comes across as a brute who sexually assaults his niece and beats her when she rejects him; the only men to behave decently towards her come from the rich bourgeois household who take her in. The comparison isn't completely inappropriate, however, as the dream sequence in *La Fille de l'eau*, in which Virginie drops away as if in flight from her various attackers, resembles Jean's vision of Juliette in her wedding dress. But rough workmen such as le père Jules were more often portrayed as *la bête humaine* (as in Renoir's film of that name, with Jean Gabin, made four years after *L'Atalante*), Dickensian or Zolaesque riff-raff given to violence and drink. By contrast, though the scene is uninteresting to look at, it contains a kernel of typical contestatory independence of mind. 'C'est pourtant vrai que nous sommes des riens du tout' ('All the same, it's true that we're complete nobodies'), agrees le père Jules, when another sailor for the barge company complains how they are treated.

The brush with authority finally rouses the old man. He's now established as the mainspring of the action, both materially (in the company office) and immaterially. His role has become that of the magical helper; he whose familiars are cats can command the magic necessary to bring about the happy ending, just like a being from the other world in fairy tale. He may not look much like a fairy godmother, but in his gruff, grizzled way, with his felines around him, he's a cousin of the old beggarwomen who turn out to be powerful good witches, in stories such as the Grimms' *Frau Holle*.

So he announces to the boy that he's going to find Juliette, and with this decision the movie leaves the dimension of historical realism once again and returns to a dream dimension where magic dissolves difficulty. Just as the gramophone began to work all of a sudden, so le père Jules will be able to locate Juliette in Paris, through the unifying, emotive communion of music. He makes only a few attempts – a hotel here, a street there – until he hears the 'Chanson des mariniers' being played.

Juliette is working as the attendant selling tickets in a Pathé Chansons Palace, under the surveillance of a dour madame. The setting must have been chosen by Jaubert, who was Pathé Cinéma's director of music at the time. Its early jukeboxes, glass booths, brass dials, dangling earphones and polished irregular surfaces give Kaufman his final opportunity to depict the graphic strength of the city of modern life – and these early pop music machines inspire powerful nostalgia today. When the madame in her booth nods off, we see Juliette choose the 'Chanson des mariniers', drop a coin in the slot and begin to listen. Outside, the horn fixed above the door begins to broadcast the tune in the street. It's another magic horn, another talisman reconnecting love and luck, for le père Jules is passing and he's called by the song. We see Juliette remembering her life on 'L'Atalante' as she listens, with an infinitely woebegone and yearning look (those four childish wrinkles high on her brow); her head drops in sadness until, in the shiny mirror of the machine's

'The city of modern life'

metal, she sees reflected the grizzled muzzle of le père Jules. This complex frame, set up with extreme care, also functions to dispel any incipient mawkishness and to intensify the feeling of magical, even comical release: le père Jules, too, has materialised as it were in water, a messenger. Dita Parlo turns on him one of her heavenly smiles, as she walks backwards into the shot to greet him – one of Vigo and Kaufman's regular uses of this movement to suggest melting. In another surprise, the old man says nothing but simply lifts her onto his shoulder and carries her off. A small hue and cry follows them, but briefly.

In Jean Guinée's script, the ship's mate has given up hope of finding Juliette when he turns into a church and finds her there, praying. He recognises her because her hands move over the beads of her rosary as they did when she knitted on board the barge.[36] Vigo's *L'Atalante* of course rejects such ghastly pieties, and he manages to transform utterly Guinée's moralising document about proper marriage, even while keeping the same ending, in which the truant wife returns. He also managed to banish that other bane of the moralising film, sentimentality. Mysterious elements help the atmosphere of enchantment and keep the didacticism at bay, but above all Vigo suffuses the conclusion with a sweet-tempered all-forgiving tenderness. Jean, when he learns from the boy that le père Jules has gone to fetch Juliette, immediately wakes up from his catatonia, knows without doubt that he will find her and she will be back. He shaves, dusts the cabin in readiness for her return, throws the dirty laundry back in the cupboard. These reactions arise from the inevitability of a fairy tale, a genre in which the structure determines the happy outcome. Le père Jules escorts her to the hatch, she looks apprehensive; a siren's whistle blows. The old man closes the hatch. She comes down the steps into the cabin, they look at each other in silence, with a gentle, sweet seriousness, and then rush into each other's arms, knocking a table sideways. As they roll on the floor in their refound love, kissing and smiling, the women's chorus of the 'Chanson des mariniers' rises on the soundtrack.

Guinée's script had ended in brutal pessimism: no husband could ever trust a wife who had behaved like that. But in Vigo's film, as the voices sing out, with just that hint of raucous, defiant courage shown as well in Jaubert's schoolboy chorus for *Zéro de conduite*, the image cuts to a fresh, airborne view of 'L'Atalante' sailing up the screen. The camera holds the barge's ascent for a moment, then flies on ahead, and overtakes it; the image fills with the emptiness of opaque water, speckled with light, and then travels on, as if soaring. The shot itself feels like an elixir of life. William Simon commented in his fine book on Vigo that the camera itself conveys its own liberation in this last shot of 'L'Atalante': 'This is an emblematic shot – the final instance of Vigo's exercise of his imagination.'[37] The water is the symbol of time, of the future – the element in which the beloved can be seen with the eyes of a true lover, a blankness and a fullness at once, the dreaming subject over which the camera can take flight.

The final shot of *L'Atalante*

'La bande à Vigo'

L'Atalante was the fourth, longest and last film directed by Jean Vigo, and he was only twenty-nine when he died, after a long struggle with tuberculosis. His early death, combined with the exhilarating originality of his films, inspired comparisons with Chopin and Rimbaud and Radiguet and other geniuses cut short by illness. He was also a famous *enfant terrible*, for his first feature, *Zéro de conduite*, made when Vigo was twenty-seven, packs into forty-five minutes more genuine rebellion against authority than any more considered statement, and was immediately banned by the censors and did not receive a showing until 1940, when its defiant spirit was associated with the Resistance. *Zéro de conduite* is the founding child partisan movie, and it continues to spring a tonic series of surprises: its centrepiece, the riot in the dormitory, when in a shower of feathers the boys in their nightshirts process as if in a religious ceremony in slow motion, has still not been surpassed for sheer anarchic high spirits. But it was not, in many ways, a surprising film for Jean Vigo to make. His personal history had led directly to *Zéro de conduite*; it is autobiographical in some of its episodes and personalities, and urgently personal in its message.

Jean Vigo's father died in the clinic of the prison at Fresnes, strangled with his bootlaces. It was 1917, and Jean was twelve years old. He had been out, the afternoon of the arrest, to buy his father the laces that were used. This was not a detail he knew at the time, but he did learn it later from a book. Michel Simon commented in a radio programme about Vigo, 'Jean Vigo was eaten up with a personal drama which was his father's. ... It was [like] Hamlet. ... Hamlet wanted to avenge his father, that was it.'[38]

The circumstances of the alleged suicide have never been cleared up, but the death of Jean Vigo's father marked the climax of a complicated dirty tricks campaign called the *affaire* of *Le Bonnet Rouge*. Vigo's father was born Eugène Vigo, but gave himself the name Miguel Almereyda as a *nom de guerre*. It was a pun on 'Il y a de la merde' ('Something stinks'), and as a journalist he had once run a notorious headline – 'Je vous dis merde' ('Fuck you!') – to the

Zéro de conduite (1933): the sissy as hero

government of the day. The tactics of obscenity, with their connections to Surrealism, made their way directly into *Zéro de conduite* and Tabard's act of defiance.

Miguel Almereyda came from a noble family of Andorra, and he was proud of his Catalan roots. But his grandfather would not recognise his son's marriage to Miguel's mother, Aimée Salles, whom he considered beneath the Vigos in birth, and cut off the young family. Aimée was soon a widow, however, and when she remarried – to Gabriel Aubès, a photographer – her fifteen-year-old son left home for Paris, where he joined anarchist circles and was soon in trouble for borrowing his rent from his employer's cash box. Sentenced to the reform prison for young offenders at La Petite Roquette, Eugène Vigo suffered there the stupidity, discipline and cowardly oppressions of the authorities, which his son captures in *Zéro de conduite*. It was after the youth was discharged that he changed his name, returned to Paris, and began writing for anarchist papers. Arrested again, for making a small bomb in a shoe polish tin and planting it in a pissoir (where it failed to go off), Almereyda, now seventeen, was sent to prison and kept in solitary confinement for a year in darkness and semi-silence.

Some of his political contacts were staunch, and the young man was helped, on leaving prison, to set up again in Paris. His mother had meanwhile been committed to a mental institution, where she soon died. After a spell of photography, Miguel Almereyda returned to journalism and began making his mark at *Le Libertaire*, an anarchist paper. In 1903, he met Emily Cléro, an anarchist activist, and she left her former partner and her four children to live with him. One night, when they were all out drinking, Almereyda invited his friends back to see the new arrival. The friends expected to find another litter, as the couple lived with lots of cats, but instead they met a baby, Jean Vigo, whom no one – not even Emily, it's said – had been aware was on the way.

Jean Vigo was born on 26 April 1905, and his advent was considered 'a miracle of comedy'.[39] Politics with his mother's milk –

and his father's (he was bottle-fed by him at meetings) – infant attendance at demonstrations, nurses and minders who were kind-hearted ex-communards, militants and revolutionaries, regular disappearances of his father to prison – none of this made a hard lad of Jean Vigo. His disrupted and disaster-strewn upbringing even provided him later with a wide circle of contacts, a kind of alternative family – Fanny Clar, for instance, who plays Juliette's mother in the wedding scene in *L'Atalante*, was a journalist on *Le Soir* and a close, anarchist friend of Almereyda's. After his death, she helped his son when he came to Paris.

The story of Miguel Almereyda reads like a lost part of *The Secret Agent*.[40] Throughout Vigo's childhood his father was involved in attempting to unite the various revolutionary factions who teemed in France into one powerful movement, but the attempt was doomed and in 1912 Almereyda broke with his anarchist friends and joined the Socialists. He had helped bring his paper, *La Guerre Sociale*, a surprising 50,000 readers, and in 1913 he became editor-in-chief of a new satirical weekly, *Le Bonnet Rouge*. The paper was destined to have an extremely chequered existence – between July 1916 and July 1917, when it was finally closed down, 1,076 of its articles were blanked out by the censors.[41] In spite of this the family, who had previously scraped along, began to enjoy surprising luxuries of a suburban existence – from learning to walk in one prison and spending Christmas in another, the young Vigo began enjoying the park in Saint-Cloud, drives with his parents in their new cars and fancy dress parties. The funds were passed to the paper by a government contact of Almereyda's, no less than Malvy, the Minister of the Interior. Soon, in the fraught climate of the war, suspicions grew about Almereyda's allegiances, and his old revolutionary friends fell away. Yet in his paper (a daily since 1915), Almereyda kept up his attack on the war policy and on the virulently right-wing and militant Action Française. Then, when a cheque passed to *Le Bonnet Rouge* was found to be drawn on German funds, the paper was suspended and Almereyda arrested. A week later he was dead.

During the scandal, many further accusations were made against Almereyda: that he was a pederast as well as a womaniser, a morphine addict as well as a traitor. In fact, he had begun taking morphine as a painkiller; he suffered from nephritis, and when he died the autopsy showed that his abdomen was full of pus – he had also been struggling with the agony of a burst appendix. His 'suicide' in prison made the truth of his later years impossible to disentangle, and the sequence of treason trials which followed embroiled all kinds of people from the highest echelons of French power and did nothing to elucidate Almereyda's role. Was he a German spy, an agent provocateur, a fifth columnist? In the eyes of his son, Jean Vigo, he was always to remain a deeply wronged fighter for freedom who had been murdered by his enemies.

The effect of the tragedy on the twelve-year-old Vigo was immediate, and material as well. He was sent away to Montpellier, to live with Gabriel Aubès, the photographer who was his step-grandfather, as his mother Emily had no means to support him. There, the first signs of the ill health that would eventually kill him began to show, and the doctor advised mountain air. After a short spell at a local primary school he was given a new identity – Jean Salles – to conceal the notoriety of his origins, and sent to boarding school in Millau. These four years at Millau provided him with the background and some of the characters for *Zéro de conduite*. They were followed by two more at another school, a *lycée* in Chartres, where he began to show his brilliance. But tuberculosis was already established, and in 1926, in the midst of his studies at the Sorbonne and his first attempts to get to work in film (he applied to assist Abel Gance on *Napoleon* [1927]), Vigo was sent to a sanatorium at Font-Romeu. There he met Elisabeth Lozinska, known as Lydou, a Polish industrialist's daughter who was also trying to recover from – to defeat – Pott's disease, tuberculosis of the bones.

In her photographs Lydou looks spirited and very beautiful, a gazelle-like young woman with a shock of frizzy hair, in a gauzy flapper dress in one photograph, carrying a huge, wild bouquet of

flowers in another (just like the boy's at the beginning of
L'Atalante), and in another throwing her head back in wild laughter
as Vigo pokes a long, long tongue out at her. For their health, they
went to live on the Riviera, and when they got married, in 1929,
Lydou's father gave the couple money for a wedding present with
which Vigo bought his first camera, a second-hand Debrie.

I have purposely left this short account of Jean Vigo's
background till the end of this essay on *L'Atalante* because it's so
extraordinarily dramatic that, like a shouting jacket of a novel, it can
overwhelm his work and shape the critical reception of the films and
any analysis of them. Secondly, there is the difficult question of
auteur versus *équipe*. Vigo is an auteur film-maker, on the evidence
of his idiosyncratic work, its original humour and fantasy and
concerns; but his oeuvre also illuminates the importance of
teamwork even in a film as suggestively individual as *L'Atalante*. His
life story clarifies this apparent contradiction: the crew and cast of
L'Atalante were connected to Vigo in special, profound and personal
ways. Vigo wasn't exactly a professional: he was an amateur, in the
strong sense of the word, an enthusiast, and he gathered around
him like-minded enthusiasts who were his friends, relations
and sympathisers with his strange, marginal background. The
complicated politics of anarchy, Surrealism and socialism in France
at an earlier period, when Vigo was growing up, inform the
character of *L'Atalante* not only personally, but materially. Many of
Vigo's colleagues were in some way connected to this history as well.
However, to watch – or analyse – the film in this light from the start
skims off the lovely, light-hearted, poignant shimmer of its love story.

They were a gang, really – 'la bande à Vigo', you might say:
Nounez the producer, Boris Kaufman, the cameraman, Jean Dasté,
the actor, Maurice Jaubert and Charles Goldblatt, Francis Jourdain.
They'd all worked on *Zéro de conduite* in the same capacity. But
the team on *L'Atalante* is also composed of some old anarchists
who had known Vigo's parents, working alongside new friends he'd
made in the three years since *À propos de Nice*. Pierre Merle, his

assistant, was the son of Eugène Merle, one of Miguel Almereyda's closest associates, who had always taken an interest in his son; the credits of *L'Atalante* also include Fanny Clar, the anarchists Raphael Diligent (Raspoutine) and Lou Tchimoukoff, besides. Family and friends took part, too: Lydou's sister Genya (does she appear in the background of the dance-hall scene?) and the writer Claude Aveline, whom Vigo had also met in the sanatorium.

Through such extended family associations, Vigo was able to call on support from other quarters too. When the budget ran out on *L'Atalante*, and there was no money to pay actors for the last remaining scene, at the station, the crew set to work. Jacques Brunius, the Surrealist film-maker, recalled how he was gathered up with around a hundred others by Louis Chavance, the editor. Pierre and Jacques Prévert entertained the crowd all through the night shoot with turns and tricks;[42] Pierre wrote later that Vigo was 'a fellow-traveller in the quest for human liberation'.[43] The name Vigo had a certain reach; the tragedy of his father influenced some people

Jean Vigo (right) with Boris Kaufman on the set of L'Atalante

in his favour. Albert Riéra, who had known Michel Simon when he'd been on the stage himself, took Vigo to meet him in his dressing room in the Théâtre du Gymnase, and the famous actor was attracted by the orphan son of a suspected terrorist traitor, whose most recent film, *Zéro de conduite*, had been summarily censored.

It's not known, however, how Vigo met Kaufman, except that the meeting took place in Paris in 1929, and together they began to shoot *À propos de Nice*, sometimes hiding the Debrie in a hat box, sometimes ducking down a sewer to catch a subject unawares. Vigo was uncommonly quick at making friends with people who could work as part of an *équipe*, and he gave his colleagues all the space they wanted.

He was mobile, adaptive and would seize any scrap of light or shade, according to Boris Kaufman, changing the narrative to fit the given conditions. Michel Simon clearly improvised his scenes; he

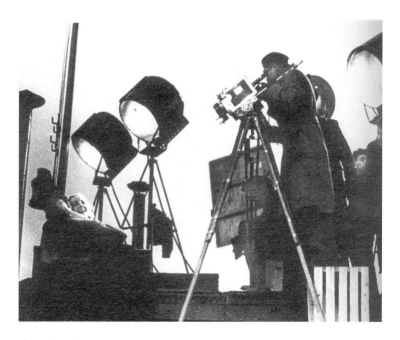

Dita Parlo on set

remembered that he and Vigo had worked up the character together, from stories Simon recalled from his background in the Vaud, and that they had filmed in one take, as Vigo, uniquely among directors, understood Simon's repugnance for retakes. Simon described Vigo himself as 'a very extraordinary, very extravagant character – Hoffmannesque'[44] – that is, a fantasist, someone out of a fairy tale. Dita Parlo said about Vigo that he was a 'natural':

I got the impression that Vigo let himself be surprised by life itself, by the scenes which came together, by the actors, the text, the light and what he saw ... we were completely free, in the middle of keeping an eye out all the time on Vigo to know whether, yes or no, that was it.[45]

She was one of the few people involved in the film who wasn't part of the gang; a professional film actress (b. 1906), German by birth, she'd had a success with *Heimkehr* (1928). But her career went into decline during the Hitler years.[46]

Furthermore, Vigo was very ill when he was making *L'Atalante* – on occasion he directed the filming from a stretcher. But he must have been someone who inspired deep loyalty, and so the film carried on, even in his intermittent absences. Louis Nounez hadn't abandoned him when *Zéro de conduite* was banned, but had remained resolved to help him make another film. With an eye on his purse, he did discourage Vigo from making one or two of the ideas he had in mind, like studies of hoboes and convicts, and thrust Jean Guinée's 'Sunday School' script at him rather firmly. Nounez's contribution was crucial to the making of *L'Atalante*; for one thing, this was the script he picked out of the archive where Guinée had deposited it two years before. At fifty-four, Nounez was twice the age of almost everyone involved in *Zéro de conduite* or *L'Atalante*, and he had had nothing to do with films before. His father was a prosperous breeder of Camargue horses, and he had become an industrialist, but he was looking for new ventures. An aficionado of Chaplin as well as the films of Jean Renoir and René Clair, he had fancied that films under an hour could fill a gap in the market. In Vigo he found someone who had a feeling for the comic, the poignant and the surreal – the fitting successor to Chaplin, Clair and Renoir. It's possible that Nounez used just such arguments to persuade Vigo to make *L'Atalante*. Nounez was also a socialist sympathiser, partly Jewish and a supporter of the opposition leader Léon Blum – the historian Theodore Zeldin emphasises the cosmopolitan connections and backgrounds of pioneer French cinéastes.[47]

'La bande à Vigo' were a puckish lot of young men and women, affectionate, optimistic, opinionated. Meeting them through the work they did together inspires today an acute feeling of our 'belatedness'. Nearly sixty years on, at the end of the century, such energy seems from another time entirely, a lost place, a vanished culture. Henri Storck, the Belgian director, is one of many friends who reported on Vigo's humour and liveliness – and camaraderie. But their relations became surprisingly, personally close: Henri Storck's mother, for instance, went to stay with the Vigos in Nice for a month and was wonderfully looked after by them. Storck also recalled heady days of telling one another 'histoires drôles', of schemes and plans, including an idea of Jaubert's to tell the story of Helen of Troy from the point of view of her butcher. De Chirico was going to do the set – great hanging sides of beef.[48]

Vigo had met Jaubert through Jean Painlevé, himself something of a prankster, who, in 1926, had filmed some incidental slapstick for the background of *Mathusalem*, a play by Ivan Gold. In one scene, Mathusalem insists on Hamlet using one of his shoes to apostrophise instead of Yorick's skull. Vigo, who as a child had been photographed in various costumes in Saint-Cloud, continued to love dressing up: one evening, he and Gilles Margaritis called on friends in women's clothes; on another occasion, Vigo and Jean Dasté were sent round to the tradesmen's entrance by the concierge at the Jauberts' apartment because they'd got themselves up to look like Communists, in red neckerchiefs and workmen's caps.[49] The editor Louis Chavance wrote that Vigo was one of the most joyful men he'd ever known, that 'everything amused him and invariably out of goodness of heart'; that he had a dark streak in his humour, too, but was never in despair; that affection for his loved ones made him hope till the very last moment.[50]

Delays had pushed the shooting of *L'Atalante* into November, December and January 1933–4, a bitter winter when ice formed on the canals. Vigo was exhausted when the filming was over, and ill; he left, with Lydou, for the mountains, where they stayed for a month. He was trying to recoup his strength to return for the final stages of the editing which Louis Chavance was carrying out in Paris. But in March, when he returned to the capital, his lungs were no better. There is some doubt that Vigo was well enough even to view the cut Chavance had made. *L'Atalante* was screened for Gaumont, the crew and the trade, but memories differ as to Vigo's attendance.[51] Distributors complained that it did not make enough concessions to popularity, and demanded changes. Some of these cuts were approved by Vigo in discussion with Chavance – they included the removal of the shoplifting scene, for instance. But when this version opened at a Gaumont cinema in Paris on 25 April, the day before Vigo's twenty-ninth birthday, it was not well received and Gaumont insisted on further changes. *L'Atalante* was then renamed 'Le Chaland qui passe' ('The Passing Barge'), after a sentimental ballad in vogue at the time, and this hit, composed by C. A. Bixio and sung by Lys Gauty, was dubbed over the credits to give the film a proper feel of schmaltz. Far worse than this, the film was drastically stripped, from eighty-nine to sixty-five minutes. Everyone involved seems to have resigned themselves with extreme reluctance to this mutilation – even Vigo, though again opinions vary about his degree of consent. When this maimed version opened in September it was surprisingly well reviewed, but failed commercially after only a three-week run.

The 1934 version of *L'Atalante*, before the cuts, was screened in July that year at the Venice Film Festival; it received little attention. This version was shown by the London Film Society in

November–December 1934, to enthusiastic notices, notably from John Grierson. The print was eventually given to the BFI; members saw it in September 1943, and it enjoyed a considerable reputation. In 1962, it was voted among the top ten films in *Sight and Sound*'s survey. David Meeker of the BFI noticed in 1988 that the BFI print was several feet longer than the Gaumont version in circulation, and in 1989 three different surviving versions were studied, combined and re-edited. *L'Atalante* was restored to its present state at a cost of 1.5 million francs. Mould still damages some sequences; computerised adjustments have removed most of the wobble from the last aerial shot of the barge, and Jaubert's soundtrack can be heard, though the same can't be said of all the dialogue.

When the new version was released, in 1990, Philip French wrote that: '*L'Atalante* is one of the most beautiful and haunting movies ever made. ... The simple story – sad, funny, humane – defines what is meant by the poetry of the cinema.'[52] It is still riding high in the pantheon of classic movies: in 1992, it ranked fifth among Directors' Best Films and was cited in a poll by film critics from Russia to Japan. Nikita Mikhalkov, the Russian director, commented: 'Everything the French nouvelle vague later achieved grew out of this film.'[53]

Vigo did not live to see his film's later fortunes. He died of septicaemia of the lungs on 5 October 1934. Lydou, who had to be restrained from throwing herself out of the window of their apartment at the time, survived him by four years before dying of tuberculosis herself on the day which would have been Vigo's thirty-fourth birthday.

Vigo was an intensely personal film-maker: he made *L'Atalante*'s tale of a marriage his own, a story of imagination and pleasure, of passion and loss. Jean fears Juliette's disappearance with an intensity Vigo knew; Lydou had been in the sanatorium for a year when he joined her there, and she was bedridden and forced to wear a corset to help her breathing. She had constant acute problems throughout their marriage – kidney illness as well as chronic bone troubles. The clarity and luminousness of passion in the film, the sympathy with fear of loss as well as real loss, draw their vividness from Vigo's own psyche. He understood 'the maze of mirrors' in which the artist who wants to represent the other finds only his own reflection. So he was stamping his own reflection, images on his retina, for perhaps the last time; the shadow of mortality infuses his knowledge of love. Felt misery and bliss lift the usual tale of erotic suffering into a realm of urgent, precise, experiential honesty about what he, Vigo, values and what he desires, and through his images we in the audience experience it too.

The Vigos were survived by their daughter, aged four; they had called her Luce, meaning Light. Light was Vigo's material, his element, his medium, his art, his effect and his legacy – in more ways than one.

Notes

1 'Close the eye of your body so that you may first see your painting with the eye of your spirit. Then bring up into the daylight what you have seen in the night.' See Sigrid Hinz, *Caspar David Friedrich in Briefen und Bekenntnissen* (Berlin and Munich: Henschel, 1968), p. 128, and a rather different translation in Colin J. Bailey, 'Introduction', *Caspar David Freidrich: Winter Landscape* (London: National Gallery of Art, 1990), p. 8.

2 Pierre Lherminier, *Jean Vigo* (Paris: Éditions PLH/Filméditions, 1984), p. 172.

3 René Clair, *Réflexion faite* (Paris: Gallimard, 1951), pp. 2–27, 111–12.

4 *Cinema Quarterly*, August 1934.

5 Lucius Apuleius, *The Transformations of Lucius*, otherwise known as *The Golden Ass*, trans. Robert Graves (Harmondsworth: Penguin, 1988), pp. 97–133.

6 François Truffaut, Introduction to Pierre Lherminier (ed.), *Jean Vigo, oeuvre de cinéma* (Paris: Cinémathèque Française, 1985), p. 19.

7 *New Yorker*, 11 May 1990.

8 Full script by Jean Guinée in Lherminier (1985), pp. 327–49.

9 Laura Gascoigne, my sister, brought this possible connection to my notice. I am very grateful to her.

10 Sally Potter, in conversation with the author, 17 January 1993.

11 *L'Atalante, Jean Vigo* (Neuilly and Cannes: Gaumont [1990]).

12 William G. Simon, *The Films of Jean Vigo* (Ann Arbor: University of Michigan Press, 1981), pp. 103–5.

13 Alan Williams, *Republic of Images. A History of French Film-making* (Cambridge, MA: Harvard University Press, 1992), pp. 122–3.

14 'We're not on board barges to have a ball/Have to graft/never leaving the helm/Going to bed late/Getting up early/Taking care of the boat.' Lherminier (1985), p. 350.

15 I haven't been able to find any other examples of this belief; Iona Opie, in a kind reply to my request for information, does not think there are any corresponding superstitions.

16 Henri Storck, in Pierre Lherminier, *Jean Vigo* (Paris: Éditions Seghers, 1967), p. 129.

17 I'm grateful to Daniel Welldon for filling in the overtones of the Spanish word.

18 'Vaches', meaning police, may have originated in occupied Alsace-Lorraine after the defeat of France by Prussia in 1870, where the German police were called 'die Wache'. See René James Herail and Edwin A. Lovatt, *Dictionary of Modern Colloquial French* (London: Routledge, 1987), p. 316.

19 'About a human being, however much one can love and want to understand, one must, I believe, renounce ever reaching the reality of them … What anguish one feels in this race before a maze of mirrors, which only yield up the image of our own image, always of our own image.' Lherminier (1984), p. 23.

20 Ibid., p. 67.

21 *Minotaure*, December 1933.

22 'One's aim will have been reached if one can manage to reveal the hidden reason for a gesture, to extract from some banal person one comes across their inner beauty or their caricature ... And do this with such strength that from then onwards the world which before we had lived beside in a state of indifference offers itself to us in spite of itself, beyond its appearance.' Lherminier (1984), p. 47.

23 It was by Léon-Paul Fargue. See *L'Amour Fou: Photography and Surrealism*, catalogue by Rosalind Krauss and Jane Livingston (London: Arts Council of Great Britain, 1986), p. 226.

24 Gilles Jacob, *Le Cinéma moderne* (Lyon: Serdoc, 1964), p. 124.

25 James Agee, '*Zéro de Conduite* and *L'Atalante*', *The Nation*, 5 and 12 July 1947, reprinted in Joseph and Harry Feldman (eds), *Jean Vigo* (London: British Film Institute New Index Series 4, 1951), pp. 13–16.

26 'Woman is the being who projects the greatest light or the greatest shadow into our dreams.' *Dictionnaire abrégé du Surréalisme* (Paris: Galérie des Beaux-Arts, 1938), p. 10.

27 P. E. Salles Gomes, *Jean Vigo* (London: Secker & Warburg, 1972), pp. 176–7.

28 Lherminier (1985), p. 351.

29 The tune was used again in *Hôtel du Nord* and *Quai des brumes* (both 1938). See François Porcile, *Maurice Jaubert: Musique populaire ou maudit?* (Paris: Les Éditeurs français réunis, 1971).

30 Lherminier (1985), p. 294. The subtitler was defeated in catching the rhymes in English patter, and so am I: 'A city that farts fire. The city that's lit on every floor…/Bikes; mopeds; convertibles for Jack-the-lad about town. It's gorgeous!/The Champs

Elysées for Baby. The Tuileries for Bibi. Notre-Dame for Madame.'

31 Lherminier (1967), p. 121.

32 See Simon, *Films of Jean Vigo*, p. 9.

33 Lherminier (1985), p. 99.

34 Conversation with Sally Potter.

35 See Ginette Vincendeau, 'The Beauty of the Beast', *Sight and Sound*, vol. 1 no. 3 (NS), July 1991, pp. 10–13.

36 Lherminier (1985), p. 348.

37 Simon, *Films of Jean Vigo*, p. 117.

38 Lherminier (1967), p. 10.

39 Francis Jourdain, quoted by Salles Gomes, *Jean Vigo*, p. 13.

40 Salles Gomes is the fullest source. See also Annie Kriegel, *Aux origines du communisme français*, vol. 1 (Paris: Flammarion, 1967), pp. 196–7, 214, and Jean Maitron, *Le Mouvement anarchiste en France*, vol. 1 (Paris: Maspero, 1975), pp. 368–71. I am very grateful to James Joll for help with the anarchist background.

41 Maitron, *Mouvement anarchiste en France*, p. 195.

42 Jacques Brunius, *En marge du cinéma français* (Paris: Arcanes, 1954; orig. 1947), p. 156.

43 Claire Blakeway, *Jacques Prévert: Popular French Theatre and Cinema* (London and Toronto: Associated University Presses, 1990), p. 36.

44 Lherminier (1967), p. 124.

45 Ibid., p. 124.

46 She was famous for her role in Jean Renoir's *La Grande Illusion* (1937) but the war seems to have ended her career in international cinema. A twist to her fame has been offered by Madonna, the star, who has adopted Dita Parlo as one of her role models – in the book *Sex* (1992), she gives her alter ego, the author of the erotic daydreams, the name Dita.

47 Theodore Zeldin, *France 1848–1945. Vol. II Taste and Anxiety* (Oxford: Oxford University Press, 1977), pp. 388–92.

48 Lherminier (1967), pp. 125–8.

49 Porcile, *Maurice Jaubert*, p. 55.

50 Louis Chavance, in Freddy Buache (ed.), *Hommage à Jean Vigo* (Lausanne: Cinémathèque Suisse, 1962), pp. 58–9.

51 Salles Gomes thinks Vigo was there, but Albert Riéra maintained that Vigo only viewed the cut made before he left for the mountains. Lherminier (1985), p. 198.

52 *Observer*, 22 July 1990.

53 *Sight and Sound*, vol. 2 no. 8 (NS), December 1992, pp. 18–30.

Credits

L'Atalante
France
First screening
25 April 1934
First British screening
November 1934

Production Company
Argui-film
Producer
Jacques-Louis Nounez
Unit Man
Henri Arbel
Director
Jean Vigo
Assistant Directors
Albert Riéra
Pierre Merle
Charles Goldblatt
Adaptation, Dialogue
Jean Vigo, Albert Riéra
From the scenario by
Jean Guinée (R. de
Guichen)
Script Supervisors
Jacqueline Morland
Fred Matter
Photography (b&w)
Boris Kaufman
Louis Berger
Jean-Paul Alphen
Music
Maurice Jaubert
Lyrics
Charles Goldblatt
Editor
Louis Chavance

Decors
Francis Jourdain
Assistant Art Director
Max Douy
Make-up for
Michel Simon
Chakatouny
Stills
Roger Parry
Sound
Marcel Royne
Lucien Baujard

Running time:
89 minutes

CAST
Michel Simon
Le père Jules
Dita Parlo
Juliette
Jean Dasté
Jean
Gilles Margaritis
The pedlar
Louis Lefebvre
The cabin boy
Fanny Clar
Juliette's mother
Maurice Gilles
The head clerk
Raphaël Diligent
Raspoutine,
Juliette's father
René Bleck
The best man
Paul Grimault
Extra at railway station

Gen Paul
Guest with limp
Jacques Prévert
Extra at railway station
Pierre Prévert
Extra at railway station
Lou Tchimoukoff
Extra at railway station
Charles Goldblatt
The thief
Claude Aveline
Genya Lozinska
Albert Riéra

L'Atalante has been
restored and reissued by
Gaumont, partly from
material preserved in the
National Film and
Television Archive.
The new version was
premiered at the Cannes
Film Festival on 14 May
1990. This is the version
acquired for the
Treasures of the
National Film and
Television Archive
collection, Its running
time is 99 minutes.
Available on DVD on the
Artificial Eye label and
from The Criterion
Collection.

Bibliography

Pierre Lherminier, *Jean Vigo*, Cinéma
     d'aujourd'hui 50 (Paris: Éditions
     Seghers, 1967).
—, *Jean Vigo* (Paris: Éditions
     PLH/Filméditions, 1984).
— (ed.), *Jean Vigo, oeuvre de cinéma* (Paris:
     Cinémathèque Française, 1985).
P. E. Salles Gomes, *Jean Vigo* (London:
     Secker & Warburg, 1972).
Henri Storck and P. E. Salles Gomes,
     'Nought for Good Behaviour: A
     Study of the Making of Jean Vigo's
     Film *Zéro de Conduite*', in Roger
     Manvell and R. K. Neilson Baxter,
     The Cinema 1951 (Harmondsworth:
     Penguin, 1951), pp. 101–30.

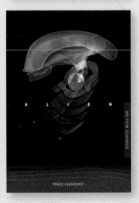